SOMETHING MAJOR

SOMETHING MAJOR

THE NEW PLAYBOOK FOR WOMEN AT WORK

RANDI F. BRAUN

NEW DEGREE PRESS

SOMETHING MAJOR

The New Playbook for Women at Work

ISBN   979-8-88504-337-3   *Hardcover*

      979-8-88504-338-0   *Ebook*

To Benj—for always believing that I was Something Major.

CONTENTS

_____

"If I am not for myself, who will be for me?
If I am only for myself, what am I?
And if not now, when?"

—HILLEL

INTRODUCTION

"Randi, I just have no desire," she whispered into the phone, worried somebody might hear her, even though she had called me from her home office.

Letting out an audible sigh, she luxuriated in a moment of relief for *finally* saying the aching, silent part out loud. "In fact," she confessed, "I honestly can't even remember the last time I was even in the mood."

It took every ounce of self-control I had not to spit out the second—okay, *third*—cup of coffee I was sipping. Placing my *The Bags Under My Eyes Are Chanel* coffee mug on the fireplace mantel, I leaned in as though she was sitting right in front of me. "Tell me everything, Ana."

"There should be sparks," she explained, "but there's just nothing lighting me up. In fact, this amazing thing happened with my boss yesterday…"

That's right: she wasn't talking about that thing you *think* she was talking about.

We were talking about work, and about a relationship to work that used to feel fresh and exciting but was different now. Ana could hardly remember the fireworks she had once felt in this job. Nothing had gone *wrong*, but things didn't seem quite *right*, either. That led to Ana looking around, asking herself, and even asking me, "Wait, how did I get here?"

She had played by the rules and done everything "right." Instead of the happily ever after she had been promised, she was left with a case of low work libido, and—unfortunately—there's just no little blue pill for that.

THE OLD PLAYBOOK FOR WOMEN AT WORK

Ana had made all the moves she was supposed to. Armed with a pristine résumé and an advanced degree from Harvard, she was six months into a new, shiny role as Chief of Staff for one of the largest tech companies in the world.

It was the job she had always dreamed of. She was working on the types of projects that could actually change people's lives—a true passion that drove her career. While her hands were calloused from her diligent climb up the corporate ladder, she rose through the ranks without martyring herself. Her hours were demanding but manageable, allowing her to balance a high-profile job, a vibrant social life, hobbies like yoga, and even a toddler. Her boss was a sponsor and an ally, and she had an incredible network of mentors and colleagues.

By her own standards, this was serious life goals material—at least on paper. But on that cold January morning, she sat in front of her computer looking at all the should-be-exciting projects on the year's strategic plan and felt unmoved.

What had once been a career that gave her "butterflies" was suddenly giving her nothing. It was an emptiness she had never experienced at work—an emptiness that left her feeling frigid when all she wanted to do was feel *hot, hot, hot*.

"This is objectively so great," she continued as she choked back tears. "So why does it feel like I wake up every day and

I'm just not in the mood for any of it?" Like so many successful women, Ana was killing it as a leader on the outside. From the inside, however, her passion for her career was slowly dying.

Ana was experiencing what psychologists call languishing: "the void between flourishing and depression."

Playing by the rules of an Old Playbook taught her a set of strategies—*"get sponsors and mentors," "manage bigger projects and budgets," "supervise more people and be a killer boss," "be a servant leader"*—but she became so lost in all the performative *doing* at work that she forgot who she wanted to *be* at work. After years of box-checking, she had never been more successful—or more numbed out to her own success.

To be clear, all those things are important. It's not that the Old Playbook is necessarily wrong or bad. It's just that the Old Playbook is way too focused on how we prioritize other people. Mentors and sponsors are critically important, but what is their value if we don't first believe in ourselves? Showing up for others as a servant leader can be transformational, but what about when we serve others at the expense of ourselves?

The Old Playbook has led too many women toward careers driven by the "shoulds." We create careers where we too often burrow inside other people's needs, challenges, and goals instead of prioritizing our own. This leaves too many of us uninspired at best (just like Ana), and burned out at worst.

The collateral damage of the Old Playbook has been insidious, and it's not just anecdotal. All we have to do is look at three trendlines in the data to see the impact on women everywhere:

#1. There still aren't enough of us in leadership roles. At the time of publication, less than 15 percent of CEOs in the Fortune 500—a bellwether metric for tracking women's representation in leadership—were women, according to *Forbes*. Of those seventy-four women, you could count the number of women of color on your hands.

These numbers are abysmal. A lack of representation at the senior-most leadership level isn't a bug in our workplaces—it's a feature: according to Lean In and McKinsey's joint *Women in the Workplace 2022* report, only one in four C-suite leaders was a woman, and only one in twenty was a woman of color.

What's even more troubling to me than the numbers themselves is the media hype. In 2021, for example, when the Fortune 500 added its first two Black women CEOs, headlines were gleeful:

"A record 41 women are Fortune 500 CEOs—and for the first time two Black women made the list," hailed *CNBC*. "The female CEOs on this year's Fortune 500 just broke three all-time records," declared *Fortune*. Yes, this is all factual information. But the story should be *why* did it take this long, *what* are we going to do to change this pace of progress, and *how* do this few women still constitute a record?

Similarly, after Black women made gains on S&P Board seats in the early 2020s, outlets ran headlines like, "Corporate boards used to be mostly white and male. That's changed since George Floyd's murder" in *USA Today* or "Black women hold record share of S&P 500 boardroom seats" in *Bloomberg*.

Hold the phone. For all the media hype, Black women's "record-breaking progress" was notching up a mere 4 percent of S&P 500 Board Seats. While these *trailblazing women* are worthy of celebration, the *metrics* aren't.

On the contrary, the fact that we celebrate these metrics instead of rallying around them as a battle cry, shows us just how broken our system is—especially when we consider that at the same moment in time, male executives still controlled ninety-nine times more S&P 500 shares *by value* than women.

> **#2. We're actively backsliding.** The COVID-19 pandemic ushered in a staggering loss of millions of women from the workforce. While many were mothers, notably not all the women who left the workforce were mothers—something that is not discussed enough.

As the National Women's Law Center found, jobs have rebounded after the pandemic, but women are returning to work at an alarmingly lower rate than men. Equally concerning is the backslide we've made in women's earning potential.

According to the World Economic Forum (WEF), the pandemic reversed the already-snail's-pace progress we were making on closing the gender pay gap. Since 2020, the WEF has extended its forecast for achieving gender pay equity by thirty-six years (the length of an entire generation), from 99 years to 135 years. Notably, that's an aggregate estimate not adjusted for the larger gap faced by women of color.

No matter how we slice it or dice it—and no matter how many Future of Work, #MeToo, or DEI stories blanket our news feeds—too many women are moving backwards in the workplace. Let me be clear: I'm not trying to bum you out.

I'm trying to keep it real about why, according to *Forbes*, 50 percent of women do not feel confident about their future job prospects.

> **#3. Women aren't happy**. This is about the quality of life in our existing system. While I'm concerned about issues like our representation in the workforce and in leadership, as well as gender pay equity, perhaps what's most troubling to me is that women aren't happy at work.

According to Deloitte's *2022 Women @ Work* survey, more than half of working women are more stressed today than they were in the past year, and nearly half of working women feel burned out. The study showed that, more than ever, working women feel like they're drowning from an "always-on" culture. In fact, a full third of women surveyed feel like they can't ever "switch off" from work. Even more troubling, the study found that nearly half of working women feel like they can't "switch off" because, if they do, their career progression will be negatively impacted. Our hustle culture is crushing women. We are not thriving. We are merely surviving.

HOW DO WE THRIVE IN A BROKEN SYSTEM?

The numbers confirm what many of us have felt all along: we go to work daily in a system that was not designed for our success. The Old Playbook was about *fixing us* to survive in a broken system. That's why no matter how high Ana climbed or how well she played the game, she never felt like she won. That's also exactly why the New Playbook is about *unlocking what's already inside of us* to find ways to thrive while our system plays catch up.

As the late Supreme Court Justice Ruth Bader Ginsburg said, "Feminism is the notion that we should each be free to develop our own talents and not be held back by manmade barriers."

But we live in a culture where we've been told that *we're* the barriers. That's why, in 2015, professors Dr. Shani Orgad and Dr. Rosalind Gill started what was known as a "confidence basket"—a place where they would toss in pictures, articles, or examples of anything they saw in media, advertising, and across the "self-help" landscape encouraging women to just be more confident.

The basket began overflowing almost immediately. So what was the problem?

Orgad and Gill saw their confidence basket, a physical symbol of "our culture's obsession with... women's self-confidence," as something bigger. Something they have since coined as "Confidence Culture."

While this kind of confidence messaging might seem empowering, it completely sidesteps the core issues of structural and systemic oppression. As Dr. Gill explains, "Confidence culture lets institutions, organizations and wider structures off the hook, because if women are responsible, then we don't actually have to make any fundamental changes."

"We're not arguing against confidence," Dr. Orgad told *The New York Times*, upon the release of their book, *Confidence Culture*. "Our criticism is of the culture that puts the blame repeatedly on women to fix what is broken in *their* self-esteem, instead of fixing what is broken in our culture."

WRITING THE NEW PLAYBOOK TOGETHER

Too much of the Old Playbook has been written with our Confidence Culture goggles on. While I certainly hope you will feel more confident after reading this book, the New Playbook is not intended to have you worship at the altar of what Orgad and Gill call the "cult of confidence." We need to move away from a place where we try to simply cheerlead and *"Yes, girl!"* ourselves to the answers when something inside of us feels broken (or at least not quite whole)—instead of acknowledging that we go to work daily in a broken *system.*

We're not letting our workplace cultures off the hook, but we also have goals and dreams that just can't wait around for the kind of systemic change we know is urgent in its need—but glacial in its action.

That's why this is a New Playbook for how women can thrive at work inside a system that is too-often designed for us to merely survive. We're in this together, so let's write this New Playbook together.

Speaking of writing, I want to go on record and say that everything people told me about writing a book is a total lie. "Oh," they promised, "it will be easy. You're not starting from scratch. You've written hundreds of thousands of words between your articles and newsletters. Think of this as putting it all together."

LIARS.

Writing this book was nothing like simply "putting content together." While this book certainly has loads of the tactical tools I've been using with my coaching clients for years, this book is really about the stories of incredible women who are *living* the New Playbook: a new set of tools and rules for building a career that inspires you, a life that fulfills you, and a legacy that impacts others around you.

…And you know what?

I'm so glad that people lied to me. Otherwise, I would have never had the courage to take on this task, and I never would have fallen in love with each and every woman's story in this book. I hope you will fall in love with these stories, too, as they inspire you by demonstrating the New Playbook in action.

While every woman reading this is a different leader and learner with a different origin story and life experience, I sincerely hope you will find yourself in this book: letting the stories and insights here serve more as a prism into the New Playbook, with its multifaceted and infinitely flexible views, rather than an old-fashioned looking glass, with its single vantage point.

What's radical about the New Playbook is that—unlike the Old Playbook, which was a linear path of box-checking—if I've done my job right, every woman who reads this book will leave with something different. That's because the New Playbook is about making your career, your leadership style, and your priorities uniquely *yours*. To that end, please think about the tools in this book as more of a buffet—sample the spread and take what most speaks to you—than a prescription.

It's about designing your rules and then playing by them in a work world we know is broken. Our world is changing, but not quickly enough. Despite it all, I'm bullish about the future, and we have dreams that cannot wait for our culture to catch up with our goals. That's why the New Playbook is all about going after them.

While most authors hope their books will be an enduring legacy, my greatest hope as a mother to a tenacious first-grade daughter is that my book will be irrelevant by the time she enters the workforce.

She's always been a part of the equation. One night when she was just two, I was tossing and turning in bed. I'd started my women's leadership coaching business in earnest and didn't even have a name for it. So I was stunned when I received an email from *Parents Magazine* saying they had heard about some bold advice I'd given on a local panel about advocating for yourself.

They wanted to interview me for an article about negotiating your maternity leave, but I wasn't sure if I should take the call. Who was I to speak to a magazine reporter? I didn't even have a name for what I was doing.

"Ugh," my husband sighed, as he sat up and said, "why don't we talk about what's bothering you so I can go back to bed."

The truth was, there was so much swirling around in my brain: the passion for this work, the fear of how much that passion meant to me, and the fear of what taking a leap away from the Old Playbook of checking the boxes on my career would mean for my life.

"I feel like I'm on the precipice of something major, and I just want to get there," I said, as we both sat in the silence that followed. Speaking those words had felt electric, and I was laying there in shock when he said to me, "You're already there. It's your move."

Every woman I've coached has also been on the precipice of *her own* something major—the idea, the project, the passion, the dream, the choice. But too often, the rules of the Old Playbook are holding us back by cutting the power on our internal electricity.

Until our world can catch up to our goals, I hope this New Playbook we co-create will empower you to navigate our broken and evolving system and go after your dreams: helping you bring yourself (on a scale of one to ten in your work life) from an eight to a nine, a nine to a ten, and then redefining your ten.

You're on the precipice of something major. Let's get there.

CHAPTER 1:

DITCHING PERFECTIONISM

———

"And I'm telling you, nobody made that Taco Bell bathroom sparkle like I could."

Working the night shift at the Taco Bell off Route 46 in Parsippany, New Jersey, was not the summer Michelle had envisioned for herself. A rising sophomore at Wellesley College, Michelle was thrilled to have her very first office job working as an intern in a fancy skyscraper. That was, of course, until the company went belly up halfway through the summer.

That English literature degree at Wellesley was not going to pay for itself, which was how Michelle found herself working the night shift at a suburban Taco Bell. Her new office was nestled between a strip mall car wash and a Roy Rogers—quite the change from a desk that, just days before, was nestled between Legal and Marketing.

The hours were also a touch different from what she'd planned. Since she didn't have a car of her own, Michelle's mom dropped her off nightly at five o'clock sharp. As her mom drove out of the parking lot in her light blue Dodge

Omni, Michelle headed into the Taco Bell where she'd work the line making tacos and burritos.

"It's been a good life skill," Michelle told me nearly thirty years later, "knowing how to fold a burrito, so everything doesn't fall out."

That wasn't the only life skill Michelle learned that summer: it was also a crash course in the hidden cost of perfectionism and overachieving.

"Because I was the low man on the totem pole the first day," Michelle recalls, "I had to do the really horrible stuff like washing all the dishes at the end of the night and cleaning the bathroom, which—at a place like Taco Bell, or really any public bathroom—is *not* the most fun job in the world."

But she did it with enthusiasm and vigor. "Because I was an overachiever, I made sure that when I washed those dishes, that nobody's ever scrubbed those pans as well as I did. When I cleaned the bathroom, it was like nobody had ever cleaned it the way I had—and I was proud of that."

Michelle was sure that her hard work—and going the extra mile in service to her self-described perfectionism and overachieving—would be noticed and rewarded.

Well, it was certainly noticed, but it was not rewarded. The next day when she arrived, her manager told her, "Wow, that is the cleanest that bathroom has ever been. It's so awesome that I want you to be the closing bathroom cleaner every night."

"Everybody had to pay their dues," Michelle explains. She was sure that when the next newbie came to their Taco Bell, she'd be relieved of her bottom-of-the-totem pole bathroom cleaning duties.

A few weeks later when a new member of the team started, Michelle was excited about moving exclusively to the more glamorous parts of the job like manning the drive-thru window or working the taco line full time. But things didn't pan out like she hoped:

> *It was an example of how being a high achiever and wanting to do everything perfectly did not yield results I liked or wanted. In fact, it backfired: I didn't get to progress up the ladder. My perfectionism made me stagnant. Management was blown away by the fact that I was the best bathroom cleaner they'd ever had, so they kept me there.*

So, as ten o'clock approached each evening, while the other employees made the night's final burritos or filled the last orders of Diet Coke, Michelle dutifully headed to the bathroom. With Billy Joel's "We Didn't Start the Fire" on cassette, she put on her Walkman headphones and cleaned that bathroom until it sparkled—and until her mom returned at eleven to take her home.

Yes, working hard is important. But what happens when we get stuck on bathroom duty in our work lives?

It's something millions of women grapple with daily even once they've made their way up from cleaning duty to the proverbial "burrito bar."

Just ask Vanessa who, after paying her dues as the Executive Assistant to the CEO of a tech start-up and becoming a global program manager, still got emails at 10 p.m. asking her to format and proofread the Board Deck because "nobody could do it better than [she] could… Oh, and could [she] order those Jimmy John's sandwiches everyone loves while [she] was at it?" Or Sam who, even as an Executive Vice President, still took the meeting notes because hers were "best in class."

Yes, doing excellent work is always an asset, but our perfectionism can too often become a liability. If this feels both recognizable *and* like a gray area, you're probably feeling the tension of the Myth of Perfectionism, which we'll unpack next.

FIVE FACTS ABOUT THE MYTH OF PERFECTIONISM

At the core of the Old Playbook is the Myth of Perfectionism: the notion that if we are perfect, we'll go further in our careers.

If we want to design a New Playbook, we must separate fact from fiction—unhooking ourselves from these mythical standards around perfectionism. Oh, and spoiler alert: this is hard work. Handling failure and embracing our imperfections are learned skills, not an end state of self-confidence-Nirvana. That's why we must start at the beginning by understanding these five facts about the Myth of Perfectionism.

#1. Perfectionism and overachieving are (incredibly) addictive behaviors. Here's the great irony about perfectionism: it's an absolutely, positively impossible standard to live up to, and yet we covet it *exactly because* it's so unattainable.

Failure to meet our perfect expectations creates a vicious cycle, accordingly. One where we (a) overachieve in the quest to hold ourselves to a perfectionist standard, (b) punish ourselves for not being good enough when we can't meet that standard, and then (c) double down on being *even more* perfect next time—beginning this self-destructive cycle anew.

Research shows that, often, the more self-doubt and self-judgment we feel for *not* being perfect, the harder we work to be better next time. This creates, in turn, a self-destructive-at-worst and utterly-exhausting-at-best pattern where we're addicted to striving for the unattainable.

#2. The Good Girl Curse is real. When it comes to perfectionism, most of us started young. Research in the field of psychology overwhelmingly demonstrates that our "Good Girl" habits are a real thing, and many of us picked up this Good Girl Curse as school children. As Julie Carrier, a former leadership consultant for the Pentagon, explains:

> *From a young age, girls are often rewarded for people-pleasing, perfectionistic behavior: being quiet, sitting still, not messing up. You plug this into an academic environment that rewards kids based on grades and SAT scores, and you're creating a reward post for girls that doesn't work in the real world.*

It's those same habits that author and psychologist, Dr. Lisa Damour, explains have made school a "confidence factory for our sons, but only a competence factor for our daughters... From elementary school through college, girls are more disciplined about their schoolwork than boys; they study harder and get better grades. Girls consistently outperform boys academically. And yet, men nonetheless hold a staggering 95 percent of the top positions in the largest public companies."

#3. Perfectionism isn't a shield; it's a weapon. We often think our perfectionism will shield us from negative feedback by motivating us to produce great work. The truth, however, is that our perfectionism is more like a self-inflicted knife wound than it is any sort of protective shield.

As my friend Claire Wasserman, founder of Ladies Get Paid, author of a book with the same title, and a self-described "work-in-progress recovering-perfectionist," said so perfectly one day when we were discussing this topic, "Perfectionism is this weird paradox: we're criticizing ourselves to protect ourselves from the potential of *outward* criticism, but it's ironic because we've actually *guaranteed* the criticism. It's just coming from *ourselves*."

Compound this with the vicious and addictive cycle we discussed above, and it's clear to see that perfectionism does more harm than good.

#4. We're trying to hit the accelerator, but we're actually hitting the brakes. At the core of the Old Playbook's Myth of Perfectionism is the notion that if we are perfect, we'll go further in our careers. Here's the reality: burrowing inside our perfectionism and exhausting ourselves with overachieving is more like hitting the brakes than the accelerator. Instead of speeding us up toward our goals, it slows us down.

It's important to remember that our perfectionistic and overachieving habits often saddle us with the office housework—the non-essential, non-promotable work that happens in our workplaces, like ordering lunch, taking meeting notes, formatting the slide deck, and organizing the birthday gift or happy hour (or in Michelle's more literal case: cleaning the bathroom nightly). Sure, being a team player is important, and *somebody* has to do each of these jobs in the workplace—but we've got a systemic issue on our hands when those *somebodies* are constantly women.

To that end, Dr. Lise Vesterlund, a professor of economics at the University of Pittsburgh, explains that women are 50 percent more likely than men to do office housework—with women of color taking on more office housework than any other population in the workplace.

> **#5. Perfectionism makes us less authentic.** In addition to bogging us down with heaps of non-promotable work, perfectionism is a barrier to authenticity. As we'll explore in even greater detail in the next chapter, when we're obsessed with how others will *see* us, we miss a crucial opportunity to *be* the best version of ourselves—often harboring a lot of self-destructive shame in the process.

As author and women's leadership expert Tiffany Dufu confesses in her book *Drop the Ball*, her overachieving standards made her feel like a sham version of herself. At work, Dufu was a non-profit executive for an organization advancing women and girls, but as a wife and mother at home, she couldn't shake her perfectionistic expectations of herself: "Professionally and publicly, I was an advocate for women's empowerment, but privately I was on Stepford wife autopilot."

We often think perfectionism is the key to *finally* spreading our wings so we can fly in our careers. But if we're not careful, it does just the opposite: it makes us move through our careers more like the cocooned caterpillar than the gorgeous and unique butterfly—something we'll talk about later in this chapter when it comes to Loss Aversion.

THE ART OF BOMBING:
WHY FAILURE MAKES US BETTER

"All you need to be a good stand up is to have a unique point of view, be funny and enjoy bombing in front of strangers," comedian Ali Wong explains in her memoir, *Dear Girls*. "If you're not willing to bomb, don't even bother."

Now a celebrity comedian, Wong never took a single comedy class. Instead, she learned how to bomb the hard way: cutting her teeth at places like San Francisco's Brainwash Cafe—a comedy club that felt more like "half laundromat, half café, full homeless shelter."

Each night, aspiring comedians would line up two hours before the club opened to sign up for a small handful of three-minute spots at the club's open mic nights. They were run by a guy named Tony Sparks, "an extremely charismatic man, who vaguely resembled Dr. Dre, but with a giant mole and a vaudevillian laugh."

Nervous but excited (but still *really* nervous) to take the mic for the first time, Wong walked onto the stage, performed her three-minute set, and absolutely killed it. She would bomb many (many) times, but that night wasn't one of them. "You're gonna be famous," she recalls Tony whispering into her ear as she stepped off the stage that night.

If you know Wong from her Netflix special *Baby Cobra*, you'd be tempted to think this was a total fairytale story after that night with Tony at the Brainwash Cafe—but it wasn't. Wong remembers waking up the next morning and pledging,

"From that day forward, I would go up every single night at a different mic and try a million new jokes: I mostly bombed—it's the only way to get good."

Years later, and with countless bombs behind her, Wong had finally "made it" and was invited to open for Dave Chappelle. The problem? The show was in Los Angeles—a city Wong despises performing in. "It can be exponentially more painful to test out new material in Los Angeles," as compared to a city like Seattle or San Francisco, she explains—where maybe an accountant was in the audience, "but Shonda Rhimes isn't."

Case in point, as she stepped on stage that night in LA to open for Dave Chappelle, Wong quickly spotted her comedy icon: Eddie Murphy.

Wong was planning to open with some new material in her "ten"—the standard ten-minute set that most comedians have for gigs like this one—but, instead, made a game-time decision. Feeling like she couldn't afford to bomb in front of her icon with untested material, she made a split-second decision to drop the ten she'd prepared and do ten minutes of her best material.

All Wong got back from the audience was crickets.

"I knew Eddie Murphy specifically wasn't laughing," Wong recalls. "Because everyone knows when Eddie Murphy is or isn't laughing: you could recognize his signature goose honk anywhere and that night there were no geese. I couldn't believe it. I ate it so hard in front of a man who made me want to start doing stand up comedy and wishing that moment that I was back in San Francisco."

The experience hurt like hell, but it didn't crush her—even if it did reaffirm her hatred of performing in LA. Wong had only gotten to the point in her career where she *could* take the stage in front of Murphy for Dave Chappelle because she'd gotten so good at bombing over the years—and learned how to be more successful from each failure:

"You'll know you're a stand up when after a spectacular bomb, you don't feel like you want to quit, but instead the opposite: you want to go up again. If you don't bomb, you'll think you're good and there's no work to do. But there's always work to do. That's the beauty of stand up. A joke is never finished."

PERFECTIONISM'S HIDDEN COST: THE LOSS AVERSION PHENOMENON

Like Wong bombing in front of Eddie Murphy, Public Relations executive, Carolina Lopez Herz, also had to learn how to fail—and it did not come easily. Also like Wong, she had her own Tony Sparks, a sponsor who had proverbially whispered in her ear, "You're going to be someone big," when she was just starting her career in PR in her twenties.

She was really talented and incredibly hard-working but, as Carolina confessed, "I spent the early years of my career terrified of making mistakes. I was good at what I did but, driven by fear, I rarely deviated from an invisible playbook."

That worked in the early days of her career as an up-and-comer at one of the world's largest PR firms. But as she began rising the ranks in less than a decade to be a Vice President for North America, that mindset did not do her any favors as a leader: "As you can imagine, as I stepped into my first management roles, some of my colleagues found that play-it-safe-mentality frustrating."

This wasn't just impacting Carolina's personal confidence or her professional development. It was impacting the thing the firm cared about most: client work. Carolina could easily see that "I wasn't stretching myself or our team," but she was scared. In fact, it was Carolina's fear of getting it wrong preventing her from actually getting it right.

She was experiencing a phenomenon called "Loss Aversion."

Loss Aversion is a system of decision-making based on minimizing failure instead of maximizing success, and according to research from Northwestern University's Kellogg School of Business, it's incredibly common. Many people who get trapped in a Loss Aversion mindset believe that success breeds success and failure breeds failure—so, of course, failure feels absolutely terrifying when it's viewed as *existential* and not *situational*.

On the contrary, the research from Kellogg completely blows up that idea, demonstrating that failure can be utterly transformative.

Like Wong and her bombing, it turns out that failure can make the careers of high-performers *even more* successful. Especially when it comes to something the researchers called "near-miss-failure"—the type of failure we experience not when we sleep through the meeting we were supposed to lead but when we put our best foot forward, and the results just weren't good enough to make it a success that one time. As my dad used to say, it's that "close, but no cigar" kind of failure.

Studying a group of promising, high-potential scientists who were applying for an important NIH grant, researchers observed that the scientists who "narrowly missed out" were overwhelmingly more likely to be more successful a decade later than the scientists who won the grant funds. "Failure is devastating," explained Dr. Dashun Wang, a member of the Kellogg faculty who co-wrote the paper with the team's findings, "and it can also fuel people."

With the support of bosses and mentors who encouraged Carolina to push herself, she started taking more risks and quickly learned that "being brave enough to make mistakes is critical to innovation."

Of course, taking risks doesn't mean permission to shoot from the hip, Carolina reminds. But it did mean taking more calculated risks. A considered, well-prepared, new pitch idea that didn't land with the client? That was one thing. Coming unprepared or sloppy is another: "Mistakes borne of carelessness should not be quickly dismissed but we must be open to mistakes that happen when you're attempting something new. It's important to be cautious when money or relationships are on the line."

Today, releasing the perfectionistic fear of her Loss Aversion is a signature part of her leadership style: "I try to be the type of manager and colleague who fosters an environment of creativity, entrepreneurship, and scrappiness. My team has had some incredible successes by not being afraid of mistakes. When we do make mistakes we allow ourselves to evaluate what went wrong, learn from it, and, in the end, let them go."

THE NEW PLAYBOOK FOR DITCHING PERFECTIONISM

Once again, letting go of perfectionism and overachieving is not a state of Nirvana you must work to attain, but an ongoing (and tough) practice. Trust me, like Wasserman (and probably you), I totally relate to being a member of the "work-in-progress recovering-perfectionists" club. That's exactly why I'm sharing these five tools for ditching perfectionism.

#1. Re-examine What's "Perfect-on-Paper." Too many women have come to me because they just don't understand what happened. They did everything right, they made all the right moves, but it doesn't *feel right*. That's because sometimes our perfectionism doesn't lead us to our goals; it leads us astray to the land of perfect-on-paper but meh-in-reality.

In fact, it reminds me of this guy I dated in college. We'll call him "Dave." Dave was absolutely, positively perfect—on paper, that is. He was cute, he was nice, he was smart, he was funny, and we shared a cultural background. He even took me on a date to Martha's Vineyard once... on his own plane... that *he* piloted! He was perfect on paper and checked all the boxes, but when it came to our chemistry, there was just nothing there. So I broke up with him.

I challenge you to think about what in your career right now is your "Dave"—your perfect-on-paper-but-there's-just-no-chemistry equivalent—and if you need to break up with it. My husband, a guy I met after Dave, has never flown me to Martha's Vineyard, and yet, our relationship is filled with the things I most authentically care about. I needed to leave perfect-on-paper to discover life-changingly-fulfilling-in-practice.

#2. Be Suspicious of Your "Shoulds." Pro tip: anytime you hear the words "I should," we are in hardcore "Inner Critic" territory—something we'll explore even further in our third chapter, *Quieting Our Inner Critic*.

Spoiler: this is a place we do not want to hang out. That's why when you hear thoughts around "I should," I want you to be suspicious of these thoughts, not immediately submissive to them. Take a moment to pause and consider if the "shoulds" are actually serving you.

Before leaping into action, ask yourself the following questions (and you can also download a printable list of these to keep on your desk at www.somethingmajorcoaching.com/book).

- What's motivating me about this "should"?
- What's lurking beneath the surface?
- What am I afraid of here?
- Where is Loss Aversion coming into play in my decision-making?
- How are "Good Girl" habits influencing my thinking here?

This isn't about denying your gut reaction to something. It's about being rigorous in starting to unhook thought-by-thought, situation-by-situation from that addictive Myth of Perfectionism, it's all-too-automatic habits, and it's Good Girl habits.

Being suspicious of our "shoulds" is essential because, more often than we'd like to admit, that perfect-on-paper-mindset doesn't serve us. Whether it's drowning us in office housework or in our destructive self-doubt, or obstructing our view with Loss Aversion blinders, we must be suspicious of the "shoulds." If we're not, they can do more harm than good.

#3. Avoid the "Right Choice" Trap. As you start to question your "shoulds," you may fall into the losing game of trying to make the "right choice."

That's why one of my favorite frameworks for ditching perfectionism comes from psychologist Dr. Pooja Lakshmin, who reminds us that in moments of overwhelm, it can be *especially* tempting to drive ourselves mad searching for the perfect answer. That's also exactly the time, Lakshmin explains, when we must be on the lookout for the "right choice" trap because "there often *is* no right choice."

She elaborates, "When you find yourself mentally spinning in this way, recognize that you have a choice in how you react to and engage with your thoughts. For example, when you fixate on finding the right answer, try saying, 'There goes my mind again, telling me there is a perfect answer.' Drawing overt attention to your mind cultivates psychological flexibility, which gives you the emotional space to question whether this line of thinking is productive, or even realistic." Identifying that we might be spinning into a "right choice" trap moment is the first step toward making a better choice.

#4. Revel When Mistakes Happen (and The World Doesn't Explode). When I was in my twenties, I worked for a large, publicly traded healthcare company where people were *very* territorial about their clients. I had no fears when it came to negotiating with clients or handling tough conversations inside a multi-million-dollar book of business. What I did have, however, was this completely irrational, perfectionistic fear of messing up my email communications. I was literally more afraid of typos or making a mistake with an email attachment than I was about the actual *hard stuff* involved in the job.

One day, I pulled a file of every single client across our company who had a specific product we sold. I filtered that list down to the forty-two people I was looking for. Then I drafted up an email explaining I was their new Account Manager and that I wanted to bring a product update to their attention. I triple-checked the spelling, the formatting, and the tone. Perfect! That's when I hit send on my Mail Merge and a message popped up on my Outlook: "Preparing to send to 4,682 recipients." I had just accidentally crafted a message and sent it not only to my clients, but every single client who had this product.

"No! No! No!" I yelled from my desk, frantically smashing Control+Alt+Delete on my keyboard. I was sweating, I was shaking, I was using every last ounce of self-control (and dignity) to not cry when all I wanted to do was burst into tears. My boss came over to my desk just as my computer crashed from attempting the synchronous sending of 4,682 emails. Relieved, I thought to myself, *Okay, well at least that will stop them from going out*. Nope. A trip to the IT desk? Nope. It took over twenty-four hours for Outlook to send them—and no matter what I did, Outlook would not stop the merge. By the time I could finally get back into my inbox, it was overflowing with notes from angry colleagues emailing me from all over the world, accusing me of "poaching" their clients.

Yes, it was messy and embarrassing. But the mess was cleaned up via a few more emails and the embarrassment faded after a few days (years later, it's just a funny story). In addition to being messy and embarrassing, it was also a gift to live through one of my perfectionistic fears only to discover that it ended up not really being that big of a deal. Bonus points: I also learned a great lesson that Mail Merges are really ineffective anyway.

#5. Celebrate Taking Risks. As Carolina reflected, it wasn't until she started taking those stretchy—and smart—risks that she really leveled up as a leader and, accordingly, found a lot more confidence and fulfillment in her work life. For Carolina, celebrating the wins came intuitively. When the out-of-the-box idea landed a huge client account, there was a team celebration. The more comfortable she got with the process of trying new things—even at the risk of imperfection—the more pride she felt when she got it wrong but had tried something innovative or creative.

That's what Lynda McGee tried to teach her students back in 2022, celebrating their imperfections and failures by throwing them a rejection ice cream party.

As the longtime college counselor at LA's Downtown Magnets High School, McGee has helped thousands of students who attend the low-income, high-performing school get into top-tier colleges.

As *The Los Angeles Times* reported, the rules of the rejection ice cream party were simple: While everyone had been accepted to college, "only seniors with *letters of denial* could attend the rejection party—and they must ritually destroy the bad news in a shredder." Plus, as a cherry on top, there was an award. Many students in the room held acceptance letters to schools like UC Berkeley and Dartmouth, but the award wasn't for the most acceptances. It was for the most rejections: "The student with the most rejections would be honored with a paper crown and $50 bookstore gift card for having the gumption to try so many times. And everyone would get ice cream sundaes."

Putting ourselves out there and knowing that we can move beyond rejection is worth celebrating. So where can you celebrate, and will you take rainbow or chocolate sprinkles? Carolina's permission to be imperfect was career-altering (even if her journey didn't involve ice cream sundaes)—something she continues to share with others. So who are the women in your office, book club, or friendship circle who can share this with you?

Because so much of our perfectionistic behaviors stem from what we fear others will think of us, we'll spend the next chapter discussing how to untether ourselves from external validation—another tool for building the rules in our New Playbook that are predicated on what *we* believe.

CHAPTER 2:

UNTETHERING FROM EXTERNAL VALIDATION

"Goddamn it, brain! Why does my negativity bias have the strength of an elite gymnast? …I suppose it's because I trained it just as hard as one."

It's a question that author, *Queer Eye* star, and gymnastics enthusiast Jonathan Van Ness asks when recounting his "unhealthy behavior [with] Twitter, which is basically just Yelp for humans."

"Yes!" I exclaimed back to nobody in particular, as I walked down the block, listening to his bestselling collection of essays, *Love That Story: Observations from a Gorgeously Queer Life*, on audiobook one spring morning.

Wow, I have never felt so seen by another human being, I thought, laughing out loud and eliciting a side eye from a passerby walking his dog. Thankfully, by this moment in my life, my brain was in much more of a walk-away-from-it-all-Simone-Biles headspace than the vault-on-a-broken-ankle-and-stick-the-landing-with-one-foot-Kerri-Strug one.

Unlike Van Ness, I've never been reviewed on Yelp (which I'm grateful for) or been tweeted about on Twitter (to my knowledge). Still, as a recovering external validation junkie, I completely understood his obsessive and spiraling fear when it came to receiving negative feedback—or even just the threat of *potentially* receiving criticism.

As a former "Good Girl" and a work-in-progress recovering-perfectionist, I'd long found positive feedback utterly intoxicating. Over the years, that constant state of intoxication insidiously morphed into a full-fledged addiction to external validation. Like any addict, I had to hit my own emotional rock bottom before I could move forward in my life.

My rock bottom came in a surprising place: a stunningly raw moment inside a glossy office building in Northern Virginia. Before my maternity leave, my boss and I were thick as thieves. Seriously, we were so close that when my house had bed bugs (don't judge—city living, baby), she offered to let me and my husband move in with her for a few nights while our house was fumigated. I looked up to her and felt close to her. But really, if I'm being completely honest, I also felt constantly validated by her continuous praise. It almost feels pathetic now, but it was where I was at.

It wasn't just her *words*; it was the entire ecosystem in which the team functioned. At the time, I was working on the business development team at a not-so-new start-up. We could hardly keep up with the hand-over-fist growth, and the "wins" were so visible. It was a fiercely meritocratic environment (at least when I first started) where promotions, raises, and punch-above-your-weight, career-defining opportunities were handed out frequently—and again, very visibly—to top performers. I often say that this one was the job that changed my life, and it did for so many reasons.

While I had a confident outer persona, at the time, I also had a completely out-of-control "Inner Critic"—that relentless inner monologue of self-doubt and self-judgment—and absolutely no vocabulary to address it, let alone any tools.

So when trusting *myself* wasn't enough to turn down the volume on the Inner Critic's fears, I turned to *trusting others' perceptions of me*—breaking, of course, what I now know is the cardinal sin of Inner Critic management (something we'll explore in our next chapter).

The need for external validation created a pattern that I'd see play out again and again for so many of the brilliant, successful, powerful women I'd come to coach years later.

It looked like this: the further my career progressed, the bigger the opportunities, and the more visible my role and accomplishments became, the more I needed the security of constant reassurance and validation.

While I was winning MVP awards, being sent to Brussels to train our European sales team, and even winning the company-wide "Pitch Off" for the best sales pitch, I secretly held this need for external validation as my deepest, darkest secret. It was my emotional Achilles heel.

It was also the first time I started to notice that the rules of the Old Playbook weren't totally serving me. The notion that I should get as much feedback as possible, or consistently look first to my mentors and sponsors, distracted me from looking at my own inner wisdom. It also made that inner wisdom feel less trustworthy or valid when I did evaluate it.

Looking within often felt difficult while I contended with the huge flat-screen televisions mounted all over the walls of our office, displaying something called The Leaderboard: a real-time ranking system that constantly crunched the numbers about where you stood in relation to both your quarterly quota goals and the other members of the team.

You know where this is going already, right? I was regularly at the top of that board—something which only fueled the external validation I was constantly getting from the executives in our organization. Their bonuses were tied directly to my performance, and, as savvy leaders, I'm pretty sure they observed that "recognition" (a.k.a. constant external validation) was motivating for me.

Yet when I came back from my maternity leave, for all the positive feedback my boss had lavished on me before my leave, it was like a switch flipped. Things weren't just cold; they suddenly grew dark and strangely personal. We'll never know why things changed, but I'm pretty sure it doesn't take a rocket scientist to figure this one out.

"You are so inauthentic, and I find it utterly grating," my boss said one Wednesday afternoon, staring at me from across the small table in her office where we'd have our weekly check-in.

I was stunned. We were discussing business—my sales pipeline to be exact—when she lobbed this insult at me (something that would become more frequent for both me and other members of our team in our one-on-ones, leadership team meetings, and what we secretly called the "9 p.m. rage emails"). Still, I was not prepared for this.

This feedback wasn't about my performance, which was so off the charts they had to redesign compensation plans because my team's over-performance was so "expensive" for the business. It was about *me as a person* and the core of my personhood.

Even though my work was never better—hey, that Leaderboard spoke its truth—I was coming to work daily and still singing for my supper: second-guessing every email, parsing every conversation, and trying my very best to win back her satisfaction and approval. Once again, looking back, this feels really pathetic. It was also, in retrospect, only spoon-feeding this unhealthy, bullying dynamic.

So when she said this so casually and callously, it literally took my breath away. I know for certain that I didn't cry in her office, but I have little recollection of how we went back to our laptops, back into my Salesforce pipeline, and wrapped our weekly forecasting meeting, which went on for another twenty minutes.

Almost like piecing together a blackout, the next thing I can remember was the *ding* of the silver elevator doors opening on the ground floor of the building. Practically sprinting across the gargantuan lobby, which ran the span of an entire city block, I barreled into the tiny dungeon that passed as our office gym. Shaking, I frantically scanned my fob, burst into the women's locker room, and grabbed one of the fluffy white towels at the entrance. Sitting on the locker room bench, I finally let out the white-hot tears that were going to explode inside my chest if they didn't come out.

To feel so "unseen" on something that was so core to who I was—the essence of my *authenticity*? Well, that was the rock bottom I needed to know that this addiction to external validation wasn't working for me anymore.

Sobbing into a towel on that bench, I suddenly thought about my then-one-year-old daughter. Just a few weeks earlier, she had been sitting on the bottom step of our staircase, playing with one of those kids' toys where you match the peg to the hole. She was frustrated, trying again and again to literally jam a square peg through the round hole.

Suddenly, she went completely still. That's when she looked up at me and, without breaking eye contact, slowly took the red lid with all its peg-shaped cut-outs, off the top of the yellow bucket. Without warning, she threw it across the living room and piled every single peg into the wide-open bucket. Lifting the bucket up with two hands, she wordlessly declared victory through a gummy and drooling smile that seemed to say: "See, I figured this out! Who needs the lid and its dumb cut-outs anyway?"

Making sure I saw her bucket full of pegs, she proceeded to have the first of what I would come to learn would be a lifetime of drop-the-mic moments. Still maintaining eye contact with me, she dumped the bucket out and filled it up again, and again, and again.

At the time, I (half) joked to my husband, like any other exuberant-first-time parent would, "Look, she's a disruptor! I'm going to tell this story one day when she invents the next Uber!"

Inside the gym that day, however, my daughter was totally my spirit guide. I had been trying to bash a round peg through a square hole for *way* too long, trying to fit my out-of-the-box-ness into the mold of other people's expectations. I was constantly editing my ideas, my words, and my actions to fit the mold of what was expected and rewarded—and this had started long before this particular job or this particular boss.

Along the way, I had rationalized that I *was* being true to myself. "I'm not changing who I am," was my reasoning for years, "I'm just playing the game: learning how the system works and working it." I'd convinced myself that everybody who knew me knew my authentic personality.

Of course this hurt, I thought to myself, now using the towel to dry my tears and clean up my running mascara. My boss was right. I actually *was* being inauthentic, and that crushed me even more than her cruel (and unprofessional) delivery.

FEEDBACK: A DATA POINT, NOT A DEFINING TRUTH

To understand how we untether from external validation, we must first reimagine our understanding of feedback. Let me be clear: good feedback can be transformative for developing our skills, talent, leadership, and goals. Too often, however, we treat every piece of feedback as though it's an immutable truth when, really, it's a data point.

The Old Playbook implored us to solicit as much feedback as possible and then implement it all immediately. Seriously, I once worked for a company whose core values included "sprint to criticism." Yikes.

This outdated mindset about feedback has kept too many women, me included, hooked on praise, terrified of criticism, and tethered to external validation.

That's why, while we should continue to be open to critical feedback, we should also be critical in *evaluating* the feedback we receive before we blindly implement it. Here are three truths about feedback to remember as you do:

#1. Feedback tells us more about the giver than the receiver. Often, it tells us more about the feedback giver's preferences, priorities, beliefs, biases, values, and goals than it does about ourselves.

#2. Feedback is, by definition, a subjective assessment. It is not an objective fact. It's a reflection of how a specific person is observing or evaluating something they see or hear from you. While it's important that we hear feedback, as well as evaluate what about it could be true or what could be beneficial to improving ourselves, we must take it as a data point—not a definitive answer.

#3. Feedback is a snapshot of a moment in time. It's a reflection of your relationship with another person, a situation, or an outcome in a specific moment in time. It's not an unwavering truth about who you are and who you will always be.

Feedback can be incredibly powerful in helping us grow. I am who I am today because of some wonderful bosses and mentors who had my back: championing me when I was successful and supporting me when I failed or missed a blind spot. I suspect you may feel the same way.

While feedback can grow us, feeling tethered to external validation from that feedback stunts us. It's also a losing game. For every piece of feedback that has grown me—from bosses, mentors, colleagues, or loved ones who had my best interest at heart—staying tethered to the external validation of pleasing a never-ending cast of characters in my life has undoubtedly made my progress toward my goals (and to the most confident version of myself) slower.

While we can work to *influence* people's perceptions of us—and that influence can be important if the person giving the feedback has the power to promote us, allocate budget dollars, fund our ideas, or stonewall something we're working on—we absolutely cannot *control* it. In fact, it's exactly the opposite: the more we attempt to control it, the more we lose our control, our power, and our sense of self.

And that's exactly where I was: sitting on a bench having an identity crisis, having learned the hard way that aligning my goals and worth to other people's feedback was a losing game. I was exhausted from contorting myself to fit my square peg through the round hole of *other people's* preferences, priorities, and values.

WHEN WE GET IT WRONG

Letting go of external validation is really hard, even when you're Claire Wasserman.

We met Claire—author, global thought leader, and Ladies Get Paid Founder—in our last chapter when she was dropping her perfectionism wisdom bombs on us. You may recall that Claire is a card-carrying member of the "work-in-progress recovering-perfectionist" club. In fact, as Claire explains, when it comes to her relationship with perfectionism and external validation, "What's most frustrating is when you *intellectually know something*, yet your behavior can't catch up with it somehow."

Claire's behavior hadn't caught up with her as she stood on the stage in Minneapolis one evening in 2017. It was a stop in the middle of her nineteen-city *Ladies Get Paid Town Hall Tour*, and those Town Halls meant the world to her.

"That's really how my business was built," Claire said when discussing how Ladies Get Paid became a global phenomenon. "Today, we're an online community touching 100,000 women around the world, but at the beginning, it was so experiential. We'd bring these women together and have peer-to-peer sharing about their relationship to money."

Claire had the choreography of her Town Halls down to a science. First, Claire would speak. Next, she'd invite a handful of "featured speakers" in each city to speak. Finally, Claire would open up the conversation to the room, asking women in the audience to pick up a mic and participate.

As she hop-scotched the country on tour from New York to San Francisco, she arrived one evening to a packed house in Minneapolis. Per usual, Claire took the mic for her remarks before passing them to the featured speakers she had selected. As her third and final featured speaker returned to her seat, Claire turned to the audience and opened it up.

"How does her story resonate with you?"

[Nothing]

"I encourage you to stand up and share a story or ask a question. Does anybody want to share?"

[Crickets]

Claire had never heard such deafening silence inside a Town Hall. Freaking out on the inside but keeping her cool on the outside, Claire pivoted to sharing another one of her own stories. As she told her story, she looked around and saw heads knowingly nodding and smiles across the faces of the women in the audience. Heartened, she thought to herself, *Maybe people just needed to feel permission to hear and see my vulnerability, right?*

Nope. As she opened it up, it was once again crickets. The audience was giving her absolutely nothing, and she was now starting to fully panic.

With another twenty minutes of programming to fill, Claire invited her featured speakers back up to the stage, moderating an impromptu panel, and counting down the seconds until the Town Hall was over. Returning to her hotel room, she was crushed.

"I immediately jumped to 'it didn't go well,'" Claire recalls about how she began spiraling. "And not only did it not go well, but I took it to the next level of catastrophizing. Not only did it not go well, but it was a *failure*."

Quickly, the inner monologue became existential. I'm really bad at this, she started telling herself. In fact, I shouldn't do this at all. Ladies Get Paid deserves a better leader.

As she sat in her hotel room, Claire was seriously considering resigning from her role as CEO based on the feedback and validation (or lack thereof) from the audience that night.

As Claire was retelling me the story, she started laughing and wanted to reassure me, "Okay, and I should mention again, literally nothing went poorly, except that people weren't participating as much as I wanted them to. So imagine my reaction when, the next day, I wake up, and I get an email from somebody telling me that the experience was—and I quote—'life-changing.' I was so gobsmacked at the difference between how I felt about it and this email that I received."

At that moment, Claire realized how "crazy," in her own words, her attachment to external validation made her feel. She had just considered quitting the successful business she founded and giving up on her life's passion because a room full of women in Minneapolis were "being what they call 'Midwest nice' and simply being polite. Literally, this wasn't about me. This was a *cultural* difference."

For Claire, this was a wake-up call: she was tethered to that validation and had spun out when she didn't get it. So as she moved on to the next city on the tour, Chicago, she took a different outlook and even stopped handing out feedback forms: "I asked myself, What are these forms doing? Am I learning from it?"

The answer was no: "Because, at that point, I really felt that I'd improved the Town Hall structure and flow as best as I possibly could. I realized I'd mostly been getting positive feedback and some negative feedback. And it just made me realize how much weight I was putting on the negative feedback."

FACT: NEGATIVE FEEDBACK
PUNCHES ABOVE ITS WEIGHT

The way the negative feedback hit Claire isn't a "Claire thing"—it's an "everyone thing" and a "science thing." While positive feedback can often give us a rush, that rush can be fleeting. On the flip side, negative feedback can often feel stickier in our brains, especially for high-performers.

According to research from organizational psychologists Dr. Marcial Losada and Dr. Emily Heaphy, we're not imagining it. In their study, it took high-performers six pieces of positive feedback to neutralize the impact of a single negative piece of feedback. In other words, that 6:1 ratio shows that "a little negative feedback apparently goes a long way," as the *Harvard Business Review* concluded when reviewing the study.

This is just one reason that, while it can be helpful, feedback can also drive our need for external validation if we don't (a) slow down to critically assess the motivations and perspectives of the giver, and (b) remember that every piece of feedback is a subjective data point, not an immutable truth.

According to Dr. Paul Green, a professor at the University of Texas McCombs School of Business, this doesn't mean that we should start "shopping for confirmation" on all the good things about ourselves to try to neutralize the sting of negative feedback. It does mean, however, that we should process critical feedback with the awareness that it has an outsize impact on our worldview, so we can try to right-size our response accordingly.

Yes, it's important to not be *defined* by the feedback we receive. But it's just as important to not reject feedback outright. Instead, we must always understand what we can *learn* from it: whether that's a data point about how people perceive us or whether that's a data point about the feedback giver's perspectives, priorities, values, or biases.

THE NEW PLAYBOOK FOR UNTETHERING FROM EXTERNAL VALIDATION

As we look toward a set of tools for handling feedback productively and untethering from external validation in the New Playbook, I want to be clear: when it comes to receiving feedback, please don't throw the baby out with the bathwater (or throw wine out with the cork, as one of my clients like to say).

That's why I choose to use the word "untethering" when it comes to feedback. The key is that we want to be attentive to feedback without being attached to it. We should cultivate the power to be discerning about it, not defined by it. Below are five tools you can use, accordingly, for designing your New Playbook for untethering from external validation.

#1. Obsess Over Your Strengths, Not Just Your Weaknesses. We live in a work culture obsessed with remediating weaknesses—seriously, look no further than my former employer and their company value of "sprinting to criticism." This kind of mindset is exactly what the Old Playbook was predicated on, and it's not working.

"With all apologies to Madonna," leadership expert Marcus Buckingham explained on the TED *WorkLife* podcast, "we live in a material *remedial* world… If we're not careful, we get people focused much more about failure prevention than about soaring."

That's why I challenge you to start obsessing over your strengths. When we start to audit and own our superpowers, we develop a reservoir of *positive knowledge* about ourselves that we can rely on when we're experiencing a confidence drought. This isn't just the equivalent of high fives and "you've got this" kitten posters; this is science.

One of the largest studies of its kind, a 2016 Gallup study of 1.2 million employees, showed that companies who relied on a strengths-optimization culture outperformed companies with a weakness-remediation culture by every key performance indicator imaginable. A focus on strengths-optimization increased revenue by up to 29 percent, decreased safety incidents by up to 59 percent, and reduced turnover by as much as 72 percent.

Understanding our strengths doesn't just enhance our performance but gives us the confidence and clarity to handle our weaknesses—without letting them be existential. Remember, negative feedback will always punch above its weight. So think of learning about your strengths and leaning into them as your own internal "endurance training" for when it does.

#2. Resist "Over-Credentialing" as a Form of External Validation. Advanced degrees and certifications can be incredibly powerful tools in driving our careers forward. Sometimes they're required to close a knowledge gap or to get us into the rooms we want to be in (e.g., you can't practice law without a JD or medicine without an MD).

One thing I've observed in my years of coaching high-performing women, however, is that if we're not careful, they can also hold us back when we use them as a form of external validation.

That's what an MBA threatened to be for Nicole. She was already the Head of Federal Government Affairs at her company and, in case you're not familiar with the lobbying industry—the local artisanal craft of my adopted hometown of Washington, DC—this is a huge job and a major leadership role.

Well-respected across Capitol Hill and well-compensated by her company, it took every ounce of my self-control not to scream, "I forbid it!" when Nicole came to our coaching session and told me she was dabbling with the idea of getting an MBA.

Why did I want to scream? Because with the sheer P&L and day-to-day priorities Nicole was managing, she could have been *teaching* at an MBA program. That got me curious about whether she truly wanted to go deep on the ins and outs of marketing and financial accounting, or whether this was something else. As we coached around this, it became clear to both of us that Nicole wanted the validation of the letters and had no interest in actually going to school.

We broke it down, and for the five plus hours a week of class and the $200,000 it would take to complete an executive MBA program over the next two to three years, Nicole could invest in other options that were more aligned with her goals of raising her profile, and developing her leadership and brand: public speaking, getting more involved with her trade associations, traveling to additional conferences work wouldn't ordinarily pay for (which was still a lot cheaper than tuition), and networking.

The more Nicole invested in these areas, the more both her profile *and* her confidence grew. A noticeable and undeniable leap in her profile was evident just in the four months it would have taken her to prep for the GMAT entrance exam and sit for it.

We must beware of over-credentialing as a way of staying tethered to external validation. In Nicole's case, going back to school when she was in a position where she could have been teaching in the program could have actually *backfired* in building her reputation. As a holder of an advanced degree, I celebrate your commitment to your professional development—*and* I ask that before you enroll for your next degree or certificate, that you check back in with your motives.

#3. The Hamilton Rule: Your Idea or Your Delivery?

"Here's the thing. *Hamilton* was like a really bad elevator pitch," Lin-Manuel Miranda told Jimmy Fallon five years and eleven Tony Awards after the smash hit show debuted on Broadway.

In 2009, Miranda was invited to perform at the White House following the success of his musical, *In the Heights*. As he was prepping, he asked the White House team if there was anything specific they wanted to see or that he should be aware of. "Well," they told him, "if you have anything about the American experience, that would be great."

At the time, Miranda had an idea for what this epic hip-hop musical about Alexander Hamilton could be—and a few initial bars of music for it. But why not go for it?

Moments before he went on stage, Miranda had a meet-and-greet with the Obamas where he gave them some background on what he was about to perform (a.k.a. his self-described "terrible elevator pitch").

As Miranda told *The Tonight Show*, they smiled politely but weren't sure if he was joking… or perhaps crazy. Looking back, he cringes in the embarrassment of the moment: "Rapping founders? I think [they] really thought it was a joke: like this Schoolhouse Rock thing? Or is this like an Epic Rap Battles of History gag?"

He could have backed out of it in that moment, reverting to his *In the Heights* score, but he went for it. As he told Fallon, "If you want to see me at my most afraid, you can watch that video [of my performance at The White House]… My eyes are constantly scanning around because I'm looking for an escape route: how do I get out of the East Wing, and where are all the exits?"

For the record, both President and Mrs. Obama are now *Hamilton* superfans. But that's only because Miranda took a chance on the *Hamilton* score, despite the implicit, negative feedback from two of the most influential people in the world—can you imagine what *his* inner monologue sounded like in that moment?

His story is one I've since dubbed the Hamilton Rule for untethering from external validation. Before you throw out an idea you have because of initial feedback, consider if it's really your *idea* or the *delivery* of your idea to your audience that they're reacting to.

#4. Pull an Elaine: Co-design and Collaborate. No, I'm not talking about busting out Elaine's infamous dance moves on *Seinfeld*. I'm talking about how we collaborate with our stakeholders when we get feedback, instead of just ac48cepting it. It's a way to untether from external validation when we get negative feedback—and it's exactly how the Elaine character came to be on *Seinfeld*.

As *The Los Angeles Times* Television & Media Reporter Stephen Battaglio explains, *Seinfeld* almost didn't get made based on early feedback from the now-iconic sitcom's earliest focus groups: "All the things that made Seinfeld quirky and interesting and idiosyncratic, these viewers just didn't get it. They thought it was boring, they didn't think it was relatable. They couldn't identify with it. They didn't think it was that funny."

When Jerry Seinfeld and Larry David initially got the red light from *NBC* on the *Seinfeld* pilot, they trusted their gut that they were onto something and refused to change the day-in-a-life premise of the show, despite feedback that it was "too niche," "too normal," and even "too Jewish."

But when it comes to feedback, we shouldn't throw the baby out with the bathwater, right? We should look for what we can learn and how we can grow, without being defined by it.

Likewise, instead of making it the hill they were going to die on or caving to the studio, they co-designed and collaborated. There were things they were not willing to change (e.g., the day-in-a-life premise). But they were open to the studio's feedback of adding a female lead; the show's pilot only featured Jerry Seinfeld (as himself), Jason Alexander (as George), and Michael Richards (as Kramer).

According to *Rolling Stone*, that's when Larry David picked up the phone and called Julia Louis-Dreyfuss, a comedic actress he viewed as a tremendous, if still under-the-radar, talent who hadn't gotten the big break she deserved on *SNL*.

By co-creating and collaborating with the studio, they added the Elaine character with the actress of their choice, whose omission from the series would now be utterly unimaginable to most. Collaborating and co-creating around feedback made their show better. It's also something we can do at work when we get feedback by asking questions like:

- Can you tell me more?
- I'm hearing you say [this], and what if we tried it together like [that]?
- Your feedback is making me think of [this], and what do you think about [that]?
- Here's what I'm thinking now that you mention this: how's that landing with you?

Collaborating and co-creating in moments of disagreement is a great way to remind your feedback-giver that you are working together toward the same goal. Questions inherently catalyze collaboration and help highlight points of agreement versus points of disagreement.

#5. Beware of "Toxic Femininity." One of the most troubling things I've observed is watching brilliant women contort themselves to satisfy stakeholders who don't have their best interests at heart, especially when those stakeholders are other women.

Before you rush to implement feedback or make a decision to win the approval of somebody important to you (or your career), consider: what are their motives? Do they have your back like some of the best bosses I've ever worked for?

Or are they perhaps disingenuous, manipulative, or, at worst, toxic? That's why, as you untether from external validation, I want you to beware of Toxic Femininity. Off the bat, you might think of this as "Mean Girls" culture, the "Queen Bee" phenomenon, or just bullying in the workplace.

Toxic Femininity is the way women push each other down in the workplace instead of lifting each other up, and it's something that many of us have experienced. As best-selling author Bonnie Low-Kramen contends:

> *Toxic Femininity comes as a result of the deeply-seeded socialization we, as women, got as young girls about how we need to behave in the workplace and what we need to watch out for. We get the message early on that men are smarter than us, and therefore, get to make the decisions. So we're taught that we need to compete with each other for the approval of men. This dynamic automatically puts us in a contentious and competitive relationship with our friends from grade school through college.*
>
> *Unless we get clear on how we've been socialized about our relationships with other females, those same competitive behaviors continue into adulthood and into the workplace. Unless somebody or something comes to break the pattern or break the*

cycle, we see adult women behaving like it's junior high. Sometimes the behaviors are so normalized and accepted, we are completely unaware of the toxicity.

Countless women have worked in a workplace dominated by Toxic Femininity, myself included (which is exactly how I found myself receiving rage emails and crying in a dungeon-corporate-office-gym). We've experienced those situations where we're bending over backward to get validation from another woman who may be in a position of power or influence over us—but doesn't have our back.

Let me be clear: you will not receive their validation and fighting for it, as I myself learned the hard way, is always a losing battle. Instead of working for their validation, I encourage you to practice the tools above... and maybe polish off that résumé. You'll never get ahead as far as you can in an environment dominated by Toxic Femininity as you will in one without it. It's scary to make a leap sometimes, but my career soared after I left that office.

While we can often be tethered to other people's beliefs about us, as well as the Good Girl, perfectionistic, and overachieving behaviors we discussed in our last chapter, we are often most tethered to our own negative beliefs about ourselves. That's why in our next chapter, we'll discuss ways to understand and quiet our Inner Critic.

CHAPTER 3:

QUIETING OUR INNER CRITIC

———

"So it's settled then: you can go shave your back now."

Cady had just gotten the tour of the minefield before her—also known as her new high school cafeteria—when she met Regina. Surveying the tables before her, there were the freshmen, the preps, the JV jocks (not to be confused with the Varsity jocks), the girls who eat their feelings, the girls who don't eat anything at all, the desperate wannabes, the burnouts, and the sexually active band geeks.

There were the "greatest people you will ever meet," her tour guide Janis said while gesturing to herself and her friend Damian. "And then there's the worst: The Plastics."

Navigating the cafeteria as The New Girl from Africa, Cady had just been accosted by a creep named Jason when Regina stepped in and told Jason to buzz off (and buzz his hairy back while he was at it). That's when a friendship was born—or rather, one of the most epic tales ever told of two frenemies.

If this sounds familiar, you're not imagining it. This isn't something you vaguely remember from high school, though it might as well be for some of us. It's from the iconic film *Mean Girls*, and it's iconic for a reason. I mean, honestly, find me a woman who can't relate to this question after going through middle school and high school:

"Raise your hand if you have ever been personally victimized by Regina George?"

Now I want you to consider if you've ever been personally victimized by yourself. If you have ever told yourself a version of this story, "I'm really hard on myself, but it's what makes me so successful," you have been personally victimized by your own Regina George: your Inner Critic.

THE INNER CRITIC VS. IMPOSTER SYNDROME

Like Regina George, our Inner Critic thinks it knows what is best for us and what will make us popular and successful. But it has its own agenda, its own rules, and its own Burn Book ready to skewer those who break those rules with crushing judgment. As Cady learned the hard way, however, all we end up with when we let the Inner Critic go unchecked is walking around a drab shopping mall in an ill-fitting pink polo shirt at best and losing all our friends at worst. So, let me ask you: is that the life you want for yourself?

I don't want that life for you either, but it isn't as simple as vilifying our Inner Critic and shooing it away—otherwise, you probably wouldn't be here with me. While our Inner Critics can be mean and even self-sabotaging (mine can be downright savage), they're not inherently evil. Our Inner Critics are our internal warning system trying to keep us safe from these five things:

1. Risk
2. Embarrassment
3. Failure
4. Rejection
5. Vulnerability

Every single one of us faces risk, embarrassment, failure, rejection, and vulnerability in our lives—especially at work. That's why it's critical to know that having an Inner Critic doesn't make us deficient. It makes us human. But just because something is normal doesn't mean it's working for us (look no further than the mom jeans comeback).

Speaking of "normal," let's rethink another term we hear thrown around a lot: imposter syndrome.

In their viral *Harvard Business Review* article, "Stop Telling Women They Have Imposter Syndrome," Ruchika Tulshyan and Jodi-Ann Burey made the now widely accepted argument that we must stop using the term "imposter syndrome" to describe the self-doubt that women—especially high-achievers—feel at work.

The issue, Tulshyan and Burey argue, is not that we must "fix women" but that we must fix systemic bias and racism in our workplaces. A culture of imposter syndrome, they write, let's those issues go unaddressed and actively propagates old tropes that have historically oppressed women, especially those in marginalized communities:

> *The label of imposter syndrome is a heavy load to bear. 'Imposter' brings a tinge of criminal fraudulence to the feeling of simply being unsure or anxious about joining a new team or learning a new skill. Add to that the medical undertone of 'syndrome,'*

which recalls the 'female hysteria' diagnoses of the nineteenth century.

Similarly, our conversation about the Inner Critic is not intended as a replacement for the systemic changes that will be required for making our workplaces more equitable. Rather, it is intended as a series of tools we can use to both cope and thrive on the micro-level while we advocate for the necessary macro changes to our workplace cultures that will allow all women to thrive.

MINIMIZING FAILURE VS. MAXIMIZING SUCCESS

It's totally normal to have an Inner Critic, but we run into huge problems when that voice gets too loud or goes unchecked. That's because every time we've ever made a move to level up, stretch ourselves, or take a chance, we've had to face risk, embarrassment, failure, rejection, or vulnerability. Usually, we face some combination of those five factors, getting so drunk off our own Long Island Iced Tea of Fear that we pass out just before the finish line to our goals—or worse, we never even start the race.

That doesn't mean our Inner Critic helps us become more "successful." To be clear: our Inner Critic is *obsessed* with making sure we don't strike out—not with making sure we're hitting home runs—and those are completely different things. Just consider Joe Sewell vs. Babe Ruth.

If you're like me, you know who Babe Ruth is, but you're thinking to yourself, *Who the hell is Joe Sewell?*

While we all know Babe Ruth as "The Great Bambino" and home-run-super-slugger, I had to Google to find the guy who had the fewest strikeouts in Major League Baseball history.

Notably, as I dug deeper into MLB history (file under: phrases I *never* thought I would say), I learned Babe Ruth didn't just hold the record for most home runs but also held the record for most strikeouts at bat. That's because he didn't step up to the plate to play it safe by hitting singles. He *literally* swung for the fences.

As Ruth recalled in a June 1939 speech at the Major League Baseball Hall of Fame, "Every strike brings me closer to the next home run. Never let the fear of striking out keep you from coming up to bat." Notably, even though Sewell was also inducted into the MLB Hall of Fame, many of us have never heard of him.

Like The Great Bambino, doing big things requires us to wrangle with risk, embarrassment, failure, rejection, vulnerability, or some combination—*yes*, that awful Long Island Iced Tea of Fear. So, while it's okay to sip it, can we agree not to get blackout drunk on it?

Neither baseball nor bad cocktails were on Alicia's mind when she got a call from the Practice Coordinator in her law firm. "Will you speak at our Annual Partnership Meeting?" he asked her. "We'd love you to lead the group's presentation this year."

Flooded with fear and self-doubt, her mouth said, "Of course!" Her mind, however, immediately began racing: "Holy crap, this is a really big stage, and I'm probably going to embarrass myself." This dizzying loop continued as the call progressed. While her mouth spoke the words, "Thanks for thinking of me," Alicia's Inner Critic asked, "Can I really do this?"

Despite rising through the ranks at one of the world's most prestigious global law firms, Alicia's self-doubt didn't diminish over the years—it only got worse. Like so many other successful and high-achieving women, with each promotion, the stakes just felt higher and higher: "I was really worried this was the moment I would get the light shone on me, and everybody was going to say, 'Oops! We didn't realize that Alicia doesn't deserve to be here.'"

"As the first Black person to be a Partner in my practice group, and as a woman and a mom on top of that, I felt so much pressure to prove that I could do this, and I just wasn't sure I could. It's one thing to be a Partner, but to be a leader? I wasn't sure about that. I felt totally safe within my practice group as the woman who is a trusted advisor to her clients *and* who wears Uggs around the office—but presenting to those old-school Partners? I just felt wildly unprepared for this moment."

This wasn't a meeting where she could rationalize away her fears with a small audience, either: "We had a lot of 'mandatory Partner meetings' that nobody actually showed up to. But people—literally *everyone*, including our retired Partners—showed up for this one."

Returning to a stack of documents on her desk and an inbox filled with requests from clients, questions from junior associates, and memos about this year's On Campus Recruitment efforts, Alicia couldn't focus on any of it. She sat there asking herself one question over and over again: *Can I do this?*

THE FIVE TELL-TALE SIGNS OF THE INNER CRITIC

Alicia was experiencing just about every classic tell-tale sign of the Inner Critic. I have asked hundreds of women ranging from Melbourne, Australia to Minneapolis, Minnesota what it sounds like when they're hard on themselves, and it sounds a lot like this:

"Everyone is going to know you don't deserve to be here."

"You're going to embarrass yourself."

"You're a terrible mother."

"Everyone is going to know you have no idea what you're talking about."

While the specifics vary from woman to woman, there are five consistent tell-tale signs that signal this negative self-talk belongs to our Inner Critic.

#1. It's mean or judgy. This is the rule of thumb: if you're saying something to yourself that you would never say to a friend, colleague, sister, daughter, or basically anybody you care about, it's your Inner Critic. Period. And, yes, "judgy" is the official coaching term for this.

#2. It plays on repeat. Our Inner Critics aren't half as creative as they are *consistent*. Just like you can set your watch to a German train, you can set your own personal self-doubt mixtape to the voice of your Inner Critic. That's why most of us can recognize the same zingers that we hear again and again.

#3. It's the news ticker. For some of us, the Inner Critic can be deafening; we can't hear anything else or focus on anything else. For others, we experience the Inner Critic more like our own personal news ticker. The "news" (a meeting, conversation, project) is playing on the main screen, but the Inner Critic's dings, disses, and dire warnings are quietly scrolling across the bottom of the screen where the stock symbols and weather forecasts usually roll.

#4. It parrots people we know or messages we've heard. Our Inner Critics often parrot people we know and the things they have said that most wounded us. For example, your Inner Critic might sound like that teacher, that parent, that toxic friend, partner, or boss—echoing things they've said or things you believe they think about you. Having coached many women of color over the years, I've also observed it's common for their Inner Critic to echo specific messages about who they have to be and how they have to act to be successful in a society that was not built for their advancement and success.

#5. It gets loud around important things. This makes perfect sense considering that our Inner Critic is our Internal Warning System. Remember, all our Inner Critic cares about is keeping risk low. It measures success by the number of times you *don't strike out*, not by the number of times you hit a home run. That's why the Inner Critic is going to get louder when the stakes are higher—whether that's as formal as a big pitch or interview, or as informal as an Instagram post. If it's important to you, odds are your Inner Critic is going to have a very loud, very strong opinion about it.

Not everybody experiences all five tell-tale signs. However, I haven't met a woman who doesn't carry around *at least one* of these as her personal, self-doubt kryptonite.

By her own estimation, Alicia was experiencing all five tell-tale signs. In the buttoned-up, super-formal world of Big Law, she already knew (intellectually, at least) why she was asked to lead: people liked her fresh, conversational, and self-described "human" style of doing things.

But she also found herself doubting that: "Being conversational and casual were already part of my brand when I came to the firm. Everyone in the industry knows that. I default to being myself, and I know that is what has made me so successful with clients." Even so, she could not pull herself out of the spiral when it came to how her global colleagues would perceive her.

THE INNER CRITIC AND THE VOICE OF REASON

Unknowingly, Alicia wasn't just hearing her Inner Critic. She heard her Voice of Reason, too. She had emotional whiplash from oscillating between, "I know that being different has been an asset. I know that being myself and my style does come off to clients as 'I'm your most trusted advisor,'" and, "Crap, I already don't look like you, I'm a woman, and now I'm not going to sound like you. Should I just be turning it on?"

Whenever women tell me, "No really, you don't understand. Being hard on myself and having these standards *is* what makes me so successful," I like to ask them to do this Voice of Reason Gut Check, which Alicia was doing in real-time. It consists of three questions:

1. Are you making statements or asking questions?
2. Are you stuck in an ultimatum (e.g., it's either a "success" or a "failure"), or are you assessing the possible outcomes and options?
3. Are you obsessing over the problems or seeking out the solutions?

Alicia's own obsessing over the (potential) problems was helpful... for a moment. At first, it was that warning of, "Okay, this stage is really big." That is, until her internal alarm bells blared so loudly that she couldn't hear herself think over them. All she could hear was, "Can I do this?" on endless repeat.

That's why it's so important to remember that the Inner Critic is a fabulous problem-*identifier* but a terrible problem-*solver*.

Now consider that difference side-by-side. Here is a list of "Inner Critic vs. Realistic Thinking" characteristics adapted from *Playing Big*, written by own Inner-Critic-Fairy-God-mother and teacher, Tara Mohr.

Inner Critic	Voice of Reason
Makes declarations	Asks curious questions
Presents ultimatums	Assesses the options
Obsesses over the problems	Seeks solutions

Now tell me, when the stakes are high, do you want to make your choices on the left side of the column or on the right side of the column?

If, after assessing both of these columns, you're still holding onto a belief that the Inner Critic makes you successful by keeping you "self-aware," you might want to consider the distinction between "critical self-aware-ness" and "self-criticism." Psychologists say that critical self-awareness is about "reality-checking the messages we hear and expectations that drive the 'never good enough' gremlins," while self-criticism is beating ourselves up for our perceived imperfections.

If you're still finding it difficult to disentangle the Inner Critic from the Voice of Reason, or self-criticism from criti-cal self-awareness, you're not doing it wrong. It's *really* hard. That's why Alicia found it helpful to personify her Inner Critic. To do so, we walked through a series of questions together. They're simple, and sometimes they can feel weird, but they can be life-changing:

1. What are the mean or judgy things your Inner Critic says to you?
2. What does your Inner Critic believe about you, the world, or what "success" means?
3. Who does your Inner Critic sound like, or what messages does it echo that you've heard before?
4. How would you describe the Inner Critic's vibe? Is it scared, anxious, happy, sad, or something else?
5. Now that you have this vocabulary, when is a spe-cific time you have heard the Inner Critic's voice before?
6. What does your Inner Critic look like?

The first question was easy to answer. Alicia was stuck in the endless spiral of, "Can I do this?"

Turning to question two about what her Inner Critic believed, Alicia laughed: "She sees success as pure perfection, and that's just ridiculous. She believes I'm not good enough to do this, but I know I can." Alicia was inadvertently stumbling upon what many women discover when they get to know their Inner Critic: yes, her Inner Critic was a great risk-identifier, but she was also kind of a ridiculously hyperbolic drama queen.

She wasn't just dramatic. "She's honestly really just scared," Alicia said, reflecting on her Inner Critic's temperament. "This is hard for me to say out loud," she shared after a long pause, "but she actually kind of sounds like me. I hear my voice. When I try to picture her, she even looks like me. It sounds so weird, but I see her as this version of me in dark blue skinny jeans and a black V-neck tee shirt with my hair in a bun and my glasses on."

"So, can we agree to wear a different outfit on presentation day?" I ribbed her.

"Oh yeah, 100 percent! I may even have to wear my signature Ugg boots; we'll be on Zoom, so nobody will even know," she burst out laughing.

As a naturally hyper-logical, hyper-analytical thinker, the exercise had been a huge stretch for Alicia—and completely game-changing in the process of wrangling her Inner Critic: "I could now put her in a box. I could see her, I could hear her, I knew her outfit. This [self-doubt] wasn't just some abstract emotion. It was an actual thing. It took that fear from an all-consuming sense of 'holy shit' to something that could be contained."

While that visualization was game-changing for Alicia, it wasn't quite as game-changing for another one of my clients, Shira.

Living 3,000 miles away from Alicia's Manhattan office and working as a product leader for a Big Tech company on the West Coast, Shira felt stumped when we walked through the same Getting-To-Know-Your-Inner-Critic Questions. A member of a women's leadership cohort I was leading, Shira sat quietly as the other women in our cohort all gushed about how game-changing personifying their Inner Critic was, like Alicia did.

"My Inner Critic just doesn't show up at work. It feels like the one place where I'm the most in control and my best self," Shira shared, shrugging her shoulders but not completely dismissing it.

Something about Shira's body language told me there was something she just wasn't saying. "So where *does* that self-doubt show up in your life?" I asked.

"Honestly," she said, followed by a long pause, "at home." Before I could ask a follow-up, she unloaded.

> *It's like, I come from this long line of Jewish matriarchs in my family—and they did everything for their family. My mom and my grandma knew all the recipes. They hosted all these elaborate holidays, and now I'm the one with the big house, and it's my turn, but I don't know how to make the damn gefilte fish for the Passover Seder. I'm not sure I even want to make the gefilte fish! I want to do my job.*
>
> *I love my job, but I just feel guilty all the time. Seriously, my Inner Critic doesn't show up at work—I'm great at work. She's like some version of a tiny, ninety-year-old Bubbe [the Yiddish word for grandma] just shaking her head at me in disapproval for not being a better Jewish mom and a better Jewish*

daughter. She's shaking her head at me for not knowing how to make the gefilte fish!

Padma immediately jumped in. A first-generation Indian-American member of our cohort who worked in private equity, Padma did not share the same life experience, but she felt so seen by Shira. "Okay, so I'm not Jewish," she laughed nervously, "and I totally hear my Inner Critic at work, but Shira, I also totally hear her at home asking me why I'm not the nice Indian girl married to the nice Indian boy by now. For you, it's your Bubbe. For me, it's my mom and my Aunties."

With some trepidation, Jackie, who ran a sprawling family farm in Missouri, jumped in next. "Listen, Shira. I don't know anything about Jewish Bubbes, and Padma, I don't know much about Indian moms and Aunties, but what you all are describing... Those pressures about who you need to be at home and with your family... Well, it sounds a lot like the rural farm grandmas I grew up around. They were *tough*, and I hear them judging me all the time when it comes to my parenting, my work—basically everything that I could be doing better."

Finally, Bari, our communications executive who, ironically, was the least vocal member of our cohort, spoke up: "Well, I have nothing to add here except that I'm glad it's not just me who has a crazy, mean, judgmental Inner Critic."

While having an Inner Critic is universal, we all experience it in our own unique ways because each one of us has a different origin story and life circumstance—two things that are constantly evolving as *we* evolve. We can experience our Inner Critics in our professional life, our personal life, and in our family life.

For Alicia, this was definitely a professional experience, and she felt a profound comfort as her presentation approached and our Inner Critic work deepened. "This isn't an Alicia thing but a human thing," Alicia realized. Separating her Inner Critic from her Voice of Reason allowed Alicia to "contain it to a box." Turning down the volume on her Inner Critic and turning up the volume on her Voice of Reason also allowed Alicia to unlock more of her individuality, creativity, and innovation as she prepared her hundred-slide deck.

Suddenly, she began to feel like she had permission to spotlight the topics that were most important *to her*—not just the practice's performance numbers. She wanted to focus a big part of her presentation on diversity, equity, and inclusion, and how the firm could have more inclusive recruiting practices. She wasn't trying to be her inner Joe Sewell and avoid the strikeout. By making the deck her own, she was channeling her inner Babe Ruth.

She was swinging for the fences—and she hit a home run. "You crushed it," a colleague told her immediately following her presentation, as the phone began ringing off the hook.

"The best presentation we've ever had," another colleague emailed, and her inbox exploded for days. Even the "old school Partners" couldn't stop gushing, reaching out to tell Alicia her presentation was "uniquely well done."

What made the success sweeter was that, even before Alicia opened a single email or answered a single call, she felt like she had crushed it on *her own* terms: "This went from being the scariest thing in the world to feeling huge for my confidence. Huge for my feeling of 'I can do this, and I can do it with my own fresh spin.'" She had shown her Inner Critic that she *could* succeed at this.

If you're like anybody else who hears this story, you are probably so excited for Alicia. You knew she could do it, even when she couldn't, right?

Take a moment to notice how easy it was to bet on Alicia. So, why is it sometimes so hard for us to bet on ourselves?

One reason is that Alicia's Inner Critic wreaks no havoc on *our* confidence or decisions, so it's easier for us to root for her than it is to root for ourselves.

A second reason is that, too often, I watch brilliant women make one critical misstep that makes their Inner Critics louder instead of quieter: seeking external validation to bolster self-confidence. This is the Cardinal Sin of Inner Critic management.

As Aimee Bateman says, "If you live by other people's compliments, you will die from their criticism." Seeking external validation to quiet our Inner Critic can actually spoon-feed it new material. All a person has to do is say the wrong thing, and your Inner Critic is at the ready, arms crossed, tapping its toes, and saying, "I told you so!" Or if your Inner Critic looks like mine, doing the epic "Told Ya So!" dance from *Will & Grace* (please Google this if you have not seen it).

Really though, who *hasn't* been through something similar? That moment when we go to the friend, the family member, the colleague, the boss, or the partner, and ask for their "advice" or "reassurance" when what we really want is their validation. When they say the wrong thing, it can feel absolutely crushing.

The former First Lady of the United States of America, Michelle Obama, reminds us, nobody can tell you that you deserve to be where you are except you:

> *I have been at every table there is—with Kings, and Queens, and Heads of State—and I can tell you that everyone has doubts. Everyone is scared that they are an imposter. [However] the vast majority of these people are amazing. We need to stop the self-sabotaging messages we tell ourselves and ask: how do we own that and start re-narrating those messages?*
>
> *If you're [a woman] at the table, you have earned your spot at the table. Period.*
>
> *You can have doubts, but don't let them consume you. You have no reason to question whether you are worthy and capable. Do the work and be bold in it. Be bold in your leadership. Be bold in your position.*

So how *do* we re-narrate? How do we lead boldly? The first step is to manage our expectations, and I love the way *Playing Big* author Tara Mohr puts this: "The day of unfailing, gorgeous confidence isn't coming. Self-doubt will always be a part of what we each work with as we take steps to play bigger. The name of the game is not eliminating self-doubt. *The name of the game is learning how to let the inner critic do its thing, without taking direction from it. The goal is to hear the inner critic's voice but not let that voice determine your choices.*"

So many of us duck out from the work of quieting our Inner Critic because we're waiting for that moment when some super-confidence will vaporize our self-doubt—the next promotion, the proper recognition, the magical-unicorn moment of self-actualization where negative thoughts will be banished—and that's just not going to happen.

THE NEW PLAYBOOK FOR QUIETING OUR INNER CRITIC
You're absolutely welcome to wait for this moment of magical-unicorn confidence, but—like anybody who has ever waited for hours at the airport on a delayed flight only to be sent home—you're probably just going to end up tired, cranky, and exactly where you started (you might even end up eating an overpriced hummus and a veggie wrap in the process). Instead, I recommend using these six tools.

#1. Get to Know Your Inner Critic. Odds are, if you're like most women I've coached, you've been *hearing* the Inner Critic for years without *listening* to its distinctive voice. Take time to get to know it. For example: which of the Inner Critic's five tell-tale signs are showing up in your life?

- Mean and judgy
- Plays on repeat
- The News Ticker
- Parrots people you know or messages you've heard
- Gets loud around important things

Take a moment to journal some of the questions that Alicia and I walked through (you can also download a printable

copy of these at www.somethingmajorcoaching.com/book)
to get to know your Inner Critic:

- What are the mean or judgy things your Inner Critic
  says to you?
- What does your Inner Critic believe about you, the
  world, or what "success" means?
- Who does your Inner Critic sound like, or what messages does it echo that you've heard before?
- How would you describe the Inner Critic's vibe? Is it
  scared, anxious, happy, sad, or something else?
- Now that you have this vocabulary, when is a specific
  time you have heard the Inner Critic's voice before?
- What does your Inner Critic look like?

Don't stress if you find that the answers to some of these
questions come up as blanks for you: this exercise is about
starting to build your awareness about the characteristics of
the Inner Critic that you recognize—not about having the
"correct" answers to a test.

#2. Get Perspective. Just like we discussed in the
previous chapter, it's critical to remember that when
we receive feedback, it's a *subjective data point*, not
an objective truth. The same goes for the feedback
we get from ourselves by way of our Inner Critic. To
quiet that voice, it's crucial to recognize that the Inner
Critic is a *perspective* on a situation, not the guaranteed *outcome* of that situation.

The more I practice this in my own life, the less I see my
Inner Critic as this authoritative figure, sitting in a white lab

coat with lots of imposing paperwork and clipboards, diagnosing the problem, and writing me a prescription for the solution, and the more I see her as a fortune teller sitting over a crystal ball. We both know her crystal ball isn't real—and yet, I'm kind of intrigued about what she has to say, even if I roll my eyes at it.

As you practice getting perspective, it can be helpful to come back to that Inner Critic vs. Voice of Reason Gut Check table, adapted from Mohr's *Playing Big*.

Inner Critic	Voice of Reason
Makes declarations	Asks curious questions
Presents ultimatums	Assesses the options
Obsesses over the problems	Seeks solutions

When you're caught in the spiral of the Inner Critic's declarations (e.g., this is going to be a catastrophic failure), shift your perspective by actively tapping into your Voice of Reason and asking a curious question (e.g., What parts of this might be strong or weak? Who is somebody I can lean on for support, guidance, or advice here?). Our Inner Critic's perspectives are too often automatic. Shifting to the perspective of our Voice of Reason is a conscious choice and one that takes practice.

#3. Get Curious. Learning to tap into our Voice of Reason can help us practice what I call the "Recognize, Reframe, Comfort" formula. It goes like this:

- **Recognize**: Using the five tell-tale signs above, practice just *recognizing* your Inner Critic: "Oh, hey. That's my

Inner Critic." This awareness is clutch because it's your reminder that *you* get to make a conscious choice about how you will handle this negative self-talk.

- **Reframe**: Instead of heaping on the self-judgment and self-consciousness that comes when our Inner Critic gets too chatty, gets curious, and reframes by asking one simple question: "What are you trying to keep me safe from?" Remember, our Inner Critic is a risk management tool, so ask yourself, *Which elements in that Long Island Iced Tea of Fear (risk, embarrassment, failure, rejection, or vulnerability) is my Inner Critic throwing up the red flag about?*

- **Comfort**: Like *Mean Girls*' Regina George, whose bullying came from her own insecurity, it's counterintuitive, but all our Inner Critic wants to know is that it's going to be okay. So how do we tell them it will be okay when they're first getting all spun up because they fear it will be a disaster? Get curious about the other options and data points. For Alicia, we explored questions like, "When is another time you've presented publicly, and how did it go?" or "What are some other ways this could possibly go *besides* the Inner Critic's prediction?" These questions allow us to *comfort* our Inner Critic who just wants to know that everything is going to be okay.

As Mohr writes about her personal approach to quieting that voice, "One of my favorite things to say back to my own inner critic: 'Thanks, but I've got this one covered.' That 'thank you' is sincere, not flippant. When I say it, I feel real appreciation for the critic's attempt to protect me from potential embarrassment or failure in these highly visible moments. In the 'but I've got this one covered,' the more mature me takes back the steering wheel, assuring the fearful part of me that things are okay."

#4. Get Real. In comforting our Inner Critic, we often realize what our Inner Critic is saying or believes is totally mean, but it's also kind of hilarious in its utterly catastrophizing, apocalyptic, self-absorbed, drama queen way. Take a hot second to ask yourself, *What is actually* hysterically funny or totally outrageous *about this?* For Alicia, what was hysterical was that she felt totally confident charging clients for her expertise but was scared to give her insights to her own colleagues for free. That's ridiculous.

#5. Give Back. Research in the field of psychology demonstrates that giving back your time and talents to others can be a powerful antidote to crisis-of-confidence moments. Taking time to share your experience, insights, talents, or time with others is proven to be the "ultimate confidence boost"—even if it's an unlikely one. So the next time you find yourself in the depths of an Inner Critic spiral, take a second to de-center yourself and give back to somebody else. Who is somebody out there who could benefit from your time and wisdom? Helping them is a way of helping yourself—not to mention all the Good Karma points and feel-good vibes you get along the way.

#6. Channel Your Inner Babe Ruth. Too much of the Old Playbook was about minimizing failure instead of maximizing success. That's why I want to challenge you to channel your Inner Babe Ruth when your Inner Critic gets chatty. Remember, our super-slugger didn't just hold the record for home runs. He also held it for strikeouts.

The New Playbook is about empowering you to make big moves, so I hope that when you step up to bat on something that is important, exciting, or just stretchy for you, you will swing hard. When your Inner Critic suggests you hit a single, consider how you can use these tools to swing for the home run. Challenge yourself with one question: where can I maximize success instead of minimizing failure? Too many of us are the Joe Sewells of our lives when, with just a little more elbow grease, we could be the Babe Ruth.

Notably, while we can work to quiet our Inner Critics, we can't ever fully mute or banish them—something that came as good news to Alicia. "I don't want her to go away," she reflected a few months after the presentation. "She's a part of me, but I do want her to know her place, to be a little quieter, and to start realizing that I'm here. What I've learned through this process is that I can wrangle her." So can you.

CHAPTER 4:

RECLAIMING OUR INTUITION

———

It started with cellulite and ended with a check for $1.2 billion.

And yes, that's *billion* with a 'B.'

Somewhere along the way from that cellulite sighting to that billion-dollar check, I found myself in a room with Sara Blakely in the early days of Spanx—the category-changing shapewear brand, which she founded in 2000.

I originally had plans to be… well, just about anywhere else besides that drab, suburban Atlanta hotel ballroom that night.

You see, I was practically dragged to this regional sorority "gala" dinner (gala was how it was billed, but that's seriously generous looking back). Arriving late in an ill-fitting gold cocktail dress, I only joined the dinner as a mandatory requirement for maintaining good standing on my membership. That basically meant that I needed to attend this dinner in order to attend our party the following Thursday night, and I was not going to miss out.

Midway through dinner, the MC introduced a woman named Sara Blakely. Unbeknownst to me, Blakely—who was both local to Atlanta where Spanx would be based for over two decades and an alumna of our sorority—took the stage as our keynote speaker.

"So it all started in 1998 when I was selling fax machines door-to-door out of the trunk of my car..." That's when Blakely began a series of crises. As a college kid with big dreams but no idea what the real world held in store, I perked up immediately.

Blakely *knew* that her life needed to be more than being a door-to-door fax machine saleswoman—but she had no idea what that next big thing was. Originally, she dreamed of becoming a lawyer. A self-described "really bad test taker," that dream was derailed when she took (and retook) the LSAT and "basically bombed it twice."

Heartbroken, and needing both a change of scenery and a new adventure, Blakely went to Disney World to pursue her next big idea: to act as Goofy at the theme park. She was again heartbroken to learn that you have to be five foot eight to be Goofy and she was a mere five foot six. She missed the Goofy gig by a slimmer margin than the LSAT, but once again, Blakely was left feeling so close, yet so far, from her dream. So she found the next best thing: "I learned I was the perfect height of a Chipmunk," and Blakely spent three months high-fiving kids at Disney as a chipmunk in Goofy's entourage.

Leaving Disney was the first step into the next phase of her career. This journey would land her on the side of the road, on a really bad day, seven years later. Following her performance as a Disney Chipmunk, she had that gig selling fax machines door-to-door for a company called Danka. "And for seven years," she recalls, "I got kicked out of buildings.

People ripped up my business card in my face about once a week."

"On one particular day, I pulled off the side of the road. I had really had a tough day, and I was like, 'I'm in the wrong movie. Call the director, call their producer, cut. This is not my life.' [...] I went home, and I wanted to set an intention for a whole new life. I wanted to reinvent my life."

Drawing a line down the middle of a page in her notebook, Blakely scratched out what may have been Spanx's first SWOT analysis (a common framework used in businesses to identify strengths, weaknesses, opportunities, and threats). Listing her strengths in one column and her weaknesses in another, one thing was crystal clear: she *loved* selling, but she didn't care at all about fax machines. So she scribbled a dream in the margins: "I wrote in my journal that night [that] I'm going to invent a product that I can sell to millions of women that will make them feel good." The path wasn't clear, but the intention was.

Two years later, she encountered a second—if not more immediate—crisis that many women can relate to: Blakley was heading to a party, and she did not like what she saw in the mirror when she put on a pair of white pants. The options were, as she recalls, "really uncomfortable shape-wear—dreadful." Then there was "regular underwear which left a big ol' panty line that we could see" or "a thong that just put underwear exactly where we'd been trying to get it out of for all these years!"

Reaching for a pair of control-top pantyhose and a pair of scissors, Blakely cut the feet out from her stockings, and the first pair of Spanx was born: "I always tell people, 'When your life is really bad, and it's really a dark time, that's usually the most fertile time for change. That's what happened to me.'" With that first pair of pantyhose and $5,000, Blakely went on to build a company that she would eventually sell two decades later for over $1 billion.

A decade and a half after first hearing Blakley tell this story, I found myself in a (virtual) room with her once again. I joined excitedly to hear Blakely speak to a professional networking group I'm a part of—this time voluntarily there and *sans* the ill-fitting gold cocktail dress and catering hall chicken. Totally starstruck, I felt myself silently scream-ing, "Oh my God, I know her!" as I hung on every word she spoke.

As the conversation progressed with Blakely's signature humor and irreverence, our group asked her the serious ques-tions we were all dying to know:

> *How did she build a billion-dollar retail business with no fashion experience?*

> *What was her secret weapon for being crowned by Forbes as the youngest self-made billionaire in 2012?*

> *How did she manage to not spend a single dollar on advertising for the first sixteen years of her business?*

Then, there was the answer that surprised me the most. "What is the secret to your leadership style?" we asked her.

Her response? Intuition.

For Blakely, her intuition drove her all along, but she didn't unlock its superpower potential until she attended a cocktail party following a coveted spotlight on *Oprah's Favorite Things*. As she recalls, that's when she found herself in conversation with two men over champagne and canapés:

> They said, 'Congratulations, you invented something!' and I said, 'Yes, I did.'
>
> And one guy looked at me, and he said, 'Well, you know, Sara, business is war.' And the other guy looked at me and said, 'Yep, I hope you're ready to go to war,' and he patted me on the shoulder.

Feeling frustrated and patronized, but not dejected, Blakely went home thinking, "'Why does it have to be war?' I had a moment where I thought, 'I'm going to do this very differently, and I'm going to be guided by a very different set of principles. I am obviously *not* interested in going to war.'"

So instead of going to war, she followed her gut. Relying on her intuition, she propelled her company into a category-defining, billion-dollar behemoth—doing it all on her own terms.

Sure, her approach was unconventional—even radical—but so was her success. To this day, Blakely credits an intuition-centered leadership style and building an intuition-first decision-making culture for Spanx's success: "Intuition is something that really doesn't have a strong place in corporate America, and I *love* intuition: it's our superpower. So I lead with intuition, [and] I gave people around me permission to lead with their intuition."

So many of Spanx's decisions were made not from the data but from what Blakely calls the "dots between the data." That place in between facts, numbers, and spreadsheets where our intuition lives is the foundation of what she describes as an unapologetically "feminine leadership style." One based on "a deep connection to empathy, vulnerability, [and] intuition." She challenges her team to use *their* intuition to go beyond the slide deck, the spreadsheet, and the forecast to consider, "What do we really *feel*? What do we really *think* about it?"

With hundreds of millions of dollars each year in revenue (and countless happy women around the world), there's no doubt that this intuitive approach has led Blakey and Spanx to meteoric success.

UNDERSTANDING INTUITION

How can we think about reclaiming intuition if we've never scribbled in our journals on the side of the road after an absolutely positively terrible day of fax machine sales? Or if we've never been crowned a self-made billionaire?

We can start by rethinking what intuition is—not as the internal computer that automatically spits out the answer to a question on demand, but as an organic, internal pull toward the answers we have inside of us. Intuition is something we can access to practice looking at those dots between the data in our lives.

As Brené Brown describes it, "Intuition is not a single way of knowing—it's our ability to hold space for uncertainty and our willingness to trust the many ways we've developed knowledge and insight, including instinct, experience, faith, and reason… Sometimes our intuition or our gut tells us what we need to know; other times it actually steers us toward fact-finding and reasoning. As it turns out, intuition may be the quiet voice within, but that voice is not limited to one message. Sometimes our intuition whispers, 'Follow your instincts.' Other times it shouts, 'You need to check this out; we don't have enough information!'"

FIVE REASONS WE'VE LOST
OUR WAY IN *KNOWING* THE WAY

If intuition is so intuitive, why can it feel so hard? It's an ironic and yet stunningly common predicament. Here are five reasons many of us have lost connection to our gut instincts:

#1. The only thing we are certain about is our *hatred* of uncertainty. Brené Brown puts it so perfectly when she says that "our need for certainty sabotages our intuition." In her extensive research on intuition and faith in the workplace, she writes in her book, *The Gifts of Imperfection*, "I found what silences our intuitive voice is our need for certainty. Most of us are not very good at not knowing. We like sure things and guarantees." Too often when we turn away from uncertainty, we turn away from the opportunity to harness our intuition.

#2. Our work worlds just move too fast. Most of us work in a culture that valorizes busy-ness, rewards overwork, and thrives off a performative productivity culture where the volume of our emails and meetings is worth more than the ideas behind them (in fact, it's so pervasive we have an entire chapter on *Reassessing Productivity & Reclaiming Time*). We have been trained, accordingly, that we "win" when we work at warp speed. Reclaiming our intuition, however, requires us to slow down long enough to get in touch with it.

#3. We're too busy looking outside to look in. Over the last twenty years, Corporate America has talked a *big game* about mentoring and sponsorship. While, yes, it has gotten us more seats at the table, there has also been a hidden fee in all the fine print. Too often, the focus on mentoring and sponsorship teaches women to look to others as sources of wisdom instead of looking for our own inner voice of confidence and insight.

#4. Emotion is a double-edged sword. Historically, men who have acted intuitively from their gut are seen as geniuses, creatives, and innovators—look no further than the canonization of leaders like Steve Jobs. Women, however, are often punished for being "too emotional" in the workplace. Internalizing that rule from the Old Playbook that there is no room for feelings at work has kept too many brilliant women away from their most innovative, creative, and intuitive ideas.

#5. We live in a work world that (we think) is allergic to mistakes. As we discussed regarding Loss Aversion in our *Ditching Perfectionism* chapter, the perceived cost of making a mistake or misstep can feel terrifyingly high. Too many women self-censor their intuition accordingly, making sure we "don't get it wrong" instead of exploring "what else could be right here?" Or, to situate it in Blakely's definition of intuition, we are so focused on making sure we get the dots of data right that we make no room for the space between them.

LEARNING TO TRUST YOUR GUT

For Megan Stewart, cultivating her intuition at work started in an unexpected place: her therapist's office.

"I was in this relationship with this guy, and I legitimately thought we were going to get married. It was very intense," she recalls of how she was reeling from that type of coming-of-age-bad-break-up you can only experience in your twenties.

The more time she spent mourning the breakup, the more she realized she hadn't lost her relationship with him. She had lost her relationship with herself: "What I realized was that somewhere in the relationship—and I think it happens to a lot of us—I really lost a sense of who I was. Outside of the relationship, I had lost my innate self-confidence."

It happened insidiously, one small conversation at a time. Before she knew it, all of her day-to-day choices were being made to satisfy *his* needs and priorities—or at least what she perceived to be his needs and priorities. Megan had completely stopped making decisions based on her gut. Instead of considering what she wanted or needed was caught in a constant spiral of evaluating what *he* would want and need. Like being in the eye of the hurricane, she was so in the center of the emotional storm she could barely feel it, and yet, it was all around her.

Week after week, Megan came to therapy after work and sat down in the chair: "The number one thing we worked on was me trusting my gut—trusting my intuition about things—and I learned it was a very practiced skill."

As Megan explains, "You know how when you're learning to ride a bike, the more you do it, the better your balance gets, the faster you get, the more you recognize how it's supposed to feel? What I learned is that you have to practice using your intuition to reclaim it and trust it. It's not like it just appeared one day, and I was like, 'Oh, okay I'm just going to go with this.' This is something I've worked on a lot for years,"—and it paid off.

Years later, she discovered her intuition was showing up constantly in a new and unexpected place: work.

It was here that Megan found herself working in the Office of the Chairman for a large publicly traded healthcare company—the place where we first met. Serving as a member of what was known internally as "Save Team," Megan had one job responsibility: save at-risk business either when the client gave a termination notice or when an Account Manager warned that one might be on the way. As Megan explains, "My job was basically to go in and figure out what the root cause of the problem was and if we could turn it around to retain their business."

Functioning as a corporate firefighter, Megan crisscrossed the country, traveling four to five days a week to meet clients who were less than thrilled to see her. Megan had learned from her training that there was a formulaic way to do this: (1) get the inside scoop from the Account Manager on the problems, (2) give a PowerPoint presentation on her proposed solution for the client, and (3) provide them with a printed proposal they could sign to renew their contract or at least retain a part of it:

> *I remember sitting on these plane rides, reviewing the notes about how they were utilizing our services and thinking to myself: 'I'm walking into a room where these people have already made up their mind that they don't want our business, and I'm reading the files of how they've used us, or haven't used us.'*

I know what these services cost, and I'm thinking to myself, 'I honestly don't blame you.' With this approach, I wouldn't want to renew us either.

Adding insult to injury were the power dynamics: "Mind you, these were almost always rooms of older, white, male hospital executives, and I was thirty, blonde, and petite—the age of some of their daughters. I was also raised southern with messages like 'be respectful, don't talk back, and do as you're told.' So, yeah I was so nervous." That was until she started doing things her own way.

Megan started walking into the board rooms without a pitch deck or a proposal: "I always had them in my bag in case they felt necessary, but I'd say I only took them out ten to fifteen percent of the time." Instead of walking into the room armed with her slide clicker, she started walking in primed for conversation. "I just wanted to get them talking," she says.

For the first fifteen to twenty minutes, Megan would simply listen to both the client and her own intuition: "I can't explain it, but something would just click as I was listening because I had a really strong sense of our business and our resources, and now, I had a really strong understanding of their concern. I could say to them, 'I actually get that what we're doing is not working for you,' and I could propose a new solution."

Her secret weapon wasn't walking in with the answer but giving herself permission to ask curious questions—both of the client and of herself. She explains, "I really believed that trusting my gut—going in there to listen instead of putting a proposal down in front of them—would reveal the answer. It was the best thing I ever did because it was how I got all my sales, all of my saves."

The "Second Brain" and the Science of "Gut Feeling"

If you've ever had a "gut feeling," you are not imagining it.

Research is rapidly evolving around the science of our body's "second brain," the gut—or, more specifically, the 100 million+ nerve cells that line our gastrointestinal tract and which make up our Enteric Nervous System (the ENS).

Dr. Jay Pasricha, Director of the Johns Hopkins Center for Neurogastroenterology and an internationally recognized expert, explains that the ENS allows our gut to function as a second, smaller brain in addition to serving its primary purpose: managing digestion.

While the ENS "doesn't seem capable of thought as we know it," he explains, "it communicates back and forth with our big brain—with profound results."

More and more, researchers like Pasricha are discovering the intricacies of how "our 'two brains' talk to each other," and beginning to demystify the connection between our gut and our emotions. With more research on the horizon, expect to hear more about the science of gut feeling in the future.

Thousands of frequent flier miles and millions of dollars in revenue later, the company's leaders were thrilled with Megan. But, more importantly to her, "It was the clients that were really so much happier. It was a huge learning experience for me in the power of trusting my gut at work."

What started as nerve-wracking now felt stunningly second nature: "What I learned is that *not* following your intuition or trusting your gut is like pushing a cream puff through a keyhole: it doesn't fit, and it's just messy."

THE NEW PLAYBOOK FOR
RECLAIMING YOUR INTUITION

As Elle Woods famously explained in the movie *Legally Blonde* when using a gut feeling about a bad perm to save the day, "The rules of hair care are simple and finite. Any Cosmo girl would have known."

If only the rules were as easy for reclaiming our intuition as they (apparently) are for hair care. While our intuition is—by definition—infinite, below are four tools to get started in a more finite way.

#1. Take a Beat (According to a Nobel Prize Winner). Too often, we sacrifice our best ideas in the name of "efficiency," reacting at warp speed instead of slowing down long enough to respond. As Megan recounted, slowing down long enough to *listen*—not just act— was the critical first step for tapping into her best ideas. Spending the first ten to fifteen minutes of those meetings simply hearing the client out and letting the situation unfurl allowed her to pause long enough to think, process, and proceed.

Without realizing it, Megan was practicing what psychologist, behavioral scientist, and Nobel Laureate Daniel

Kahneman describes as "System 2 thinking." As Kahneman explained in his ground-breaking book *Thinking Fast & Slow*, System 1 thinking is *reactive*. It "operates automatically and quickly, with little or no effort like how your foot hits the brake at a red light without stopping yourself to say I should slow down now."

When we slow down long enough, he explains, we can unlock our System 2 thinking. This *responsive* thinking makes space for agency, choice, and concentration—three elements at the heart of our best ideas. In work worlds that move so quickly, many people, he asserts, are "unwilling to invest the effort [in System 2 thinking]."

While Kahneman and I use different definitions for "intuition," we agree on the most important element: System 2 thinking is absolutely critical to slowing down and making better decisions.

Just like Megan made cultivating her intuition a daily practice, consider practicing slowing down and making room to listen just once a day. You can select a single email, question, or project task and simply set a timer for five minutes. Take the matter before you, grab a pen and paper (or print out a downloadable worksheet at www.somethingmajorcoaching.com/book), and jot down your answers to the following questions:

- What's the first idea that's popping into my mind here?
- What do I already understand about this matter?
- What are the unknowns here?
- What are two other options for this scenario?
- Which of these do I believe will have the most impactful outcome?

#2. The "Body Check-In." Somatic therapist and author Bari Tessler says that while our minds can be in a million places at once, our bodies are the only thing that is always right here, right now. That's what makes checking in with our body such a powerful tool for learning how to access our intuition.

Is your body sending you a message that something feels "right" or "wrong" at this very moment? It's hard to know if no one has taught you how to listen. That's why I recommend you learn how to do a Body Check-In:

- Start by sitting upright in a chair, legs uncrossed, with your feet on the ground, your ankles aligned underneath the knees and your palms face down on your thighs.
- Close your eyes and begin to breathe, taking a long inhale through the nose and a long exhale through the mouth.
- Even with your eyes closed, you should be able to "watch" with your mind's eye as your chest rises and your belly expands, and then "watch" again as the exhale gently releases the chest and belly back toward the spine, and gravity does the rest of the work.
- Take a moment with your eyes closed and notice what you *feel* as you think through a situation. Is it the excitement of nervous butterflies? Is it a gnarled-up anxious knot in your stomach that something is not a great idea?

Tessler explains that our bodies contain an incredible amount of intelligence; all we have to do is practice listening:

The Body Check-In brings us reliably, gently, and compassionately back to the present moment, and back home to ourselves. It is only here and now that we can meet ourselves, understand ourselves, and transform ourselves... Turning into the content of your inner experience is a way of honoring it and yourself. This pause is, in fact, a radical act of self-love. It sends a message that you matter, and what's arising inside you deserves attention.

While Tessler's take borders on what I'd call "deliciously woo woo," consider another take on the Body Check-In from Nikki Adamson. CEO of the boutique recruiting firm Hustle Hunters, which pairs tech start-ups with underrepresented talent in tech, and a brilliant business leader I've been privileged to coach, Nikki describes how she uses her body to make intuitive decisions in work and life:

I've learned that I need to treat my body—i.e. my intuition—like a finely-honed AI system that's taking in all the data points and pattern matching as I go about my life. It took not acting on my intuition a couple times and paying the consequences to learn this lesson.

When Nikki's Inner Critic acts up around big decisions like a large capital expenditure, expanding her team, or taking on a client she's just not sure about, the Body-Check In is something that enables her to access her intuition instead of automatically giving in to the fear-driven perspective.

Megan also describes listening to her body as key to checking in with her gut instincts by simply checking in for the "ick factor versus the aura."

> When something feels 'icky,' I pause to see how I
> can lean into this and try to understand it. Even
> if I don't have the answer immediately, it's like my
> body has signaled to me that I need to slow down
> and look for one. Typically, when that's the case, I
> can come to a better solution or recommendation.
> On the flip side, when something feels 'right,' gut feel
> is almost like this aura in my body: there's lightness,
> a confidence that puts my body at ease.

As Tessler reminds us about the Body Check-In, "While it only takes a moment to learn, don't let its simplicity fool you: when practiced regularly, it is massively supportive and utterly life-changing. Pinky swear."

#3. Grant Permission to Connect the "Dots Between the Data." Shortly before I wrote this book, I was in a Zoom room with Michelle Obama when somebody asked her how she "learned" to be the First Lady.

"Nobody taught me how to be a First Lady," she laughed, before explaining matter-of-factly, "but I was a Harvard-trained lawyer, I had worked for a law firm, I had worked for city government, and I had done community relations for a hospital." Each one of these experiences taught her how to "trust myself to put it together when nobody was there to teach me how to do it or tell me the right answers."

When Mrs. Obama inventoried her skills, past experiences, and strengths, she implicitly gave herself permission to connect the dots between the data. It's similar to what Blakely challenged her team to do with her intuitive style of leadership: giving her team permission to connect the dots between the data by relying on their strengths, insights, and knowledge to close the gap on unknowns and make decisions accordingly.

Too often, we focus so heavily on the piece we're missing that we forget how to build with what we do have. We're so worried about getting it "wrong" that we underestimate how insightful our unique perspectives or new ideas can be.

That's why sometimes the biggest barrier isn't *having* the knowledge but *believing in* our knowledge. It's critical to recognize that we often know a lot more about a situation than we think we do. This isn't my opinion; this is *science*—specifically, a psychological phenomenon known as the Dunning-Kruger Effect.

If you've heard of it, you might recognize this effect as one concerning non-experts who overestimate their knowledge. But the inverse is also true—especially for many of the women I've worked with over the years.

It works like this: when we start something new and enter the "amateur phase" (e.g., the first few years of our career) we are most likely to overestimate our knowledge and expertise on that topic. Psychologist and *Think Again* author, Dr. Adam Grant, calls this "the peak of Mt. Stupid."

However, after we surpass the amateur phase, something funny happens: the more knowledgeable we are at something, the more likely we are to *underestimate* our expertise—and this is exactly where I see brilliant women too often doubting their knowledge and opinions.

Slowing down to audit the strengths, expertise, and knowledge we're bringing to a situation can be a conduit to accessing a more intuitive answer to the problem. When we focus on weaknesses and gaps, we almost never give ourselves permission to connect those dots between the data and make a gut call.

#4. Check Back on External Validation Bad Habits. By definition, making a call based solely on what others will think is an inherent block to making a call based on what *we* think. Nineteenth century Danish philosopher Søren Kierkegaard wrote, "We can only get in touch with our own source of intuition and wisdom when we no longer depend on others' opinions for our sense of identity and worth. We all tend to workshop something. The question is: will we workshop the god of opinion or the god of our own heart?"

Megan was putting Kierkegaard's poetic words to action when she chucked those pre-printed slide decks and proposals. By carving out a space to do it her way, she hadn't just followed her own intuition, she'd gone entirely outside of the company's set formula—and her boss was actually thrilled with the results.

It's an idea echoed by my friend, Marissa Fernandez, a former Chief Marketing Officer turned executive coaching colleague: "I've never bet on myself and lost." When we try to contort our ideas and contributions to fit first and foremost into the mold of other people's values, we're denying ourselves the chance to bet on ourselves. When we stay tethered to external validation, we always lose because we've lost the ability to hear our own intuition and trust our gut.

Our intuition is our agency, and every time we give ourselves permission to use it, we give ourselves permission to say, "My ideas matter." While the voice of our Inner Critics can be loud, abrasive, and hyperbolic, the voice of our intuition and inner wisdom is often softer-spoken and calm. It takes more effort to harness and listen to it, but it can be transformative when we do.

CHAPTER 5:

GETTING AFTER
YOUR GOALS

———

There is an ancient, Kabbalistic belief that every one of our words, thoughts, or deeds has the power to tilt the balance of the universe—ever so microscopically—toward good or evil.

While I can't speak to cosmic balance, I do believe that we have the daily power to make micro moves that can radically shift the balance inside our *personal* universe. I also believe that a failure to own our micro-move superpowers is what stops most women from achieving our most audacious, life-changing, and (often stunningly) doable goals.

Still skeptical? Let me take you back in time. Not all the way back to the origins of ancient mindfulness and mysticism, but to a time when *The Sopranos* was appointment-viewing, the Blackberry reigned supreme, and people thought frosted tips were a cool look. That's right, I'm talking about the early 2000s.

In addition to being a truly Golden Age in television and a dark period for men's hairstyling, it was a time when Great Britain's Olympic cycling team was good, but not great. Having scooped up one gold medal in the Sydney games of 2000 and another two in Athens in the summer of 2004, the team also scooped up a new coach named Sir David Brailsford.

Most intriguing to many cycling-world watchers, Brailsford wasn't even a professional cyclist. He was a cycling enthusiast and a successful businessman who was obsessed with the Japanese concept of *kaizen*—the pursuit of continuous improvement.

"As an MBA," Brailsford shared with *Harvard Business Review* in 2015 as he looked back on his tenure with the team, "it struck me that we should think small, not big, and adopt a philosophy of continuous improvement through the aggregation of marginal gains."

To win, he argued, "Forget about perfection, focus on progression, and compound the improvements."

Instead of focusing on a single area of performance where the team could make a 100 percent improvement leap (which was downright unrealistic to Brailsford), he started experimenting with a hundred different places where the team could make 1% improvements. This included experimenting with a wind tunnel to optimize bike aerodynamics, hiring a surgeon to teach the team how to wash their hands better and avoid sickness-causing-germs, or even finding the best pillows and mattresses to optimize their sleeping posture—and they took those mattresses with them as they traveled the globe on the competitive racing circuit.

Brailsford was relentless, and the team experimented constantly with 1% improvements. By the head coach's own account, the only thing more grueling than their training regimen was some of the tough lessons they learned along the way, like their initial (and emotionally crushing) underperformance at the Tour de France.

Despite a poor initial showing at the Tour, for the four years following the '04 Games in Athens, they continued to adjust and pivot, never giving up on their strategy of making 1% moves.

"Perhaps the most powerful benefit," Brailsford recalls, "is that it create[d] a contagious enthusiasm. Everyone starts looking for ways to improve. There's something inherently rewarding about identifying marginal gains—the *bonhomie* is similar to a scavenger hunt. People want to identify opportunities and share them with the group. Our team became a very positive place to be."

After four years of schlepping their mattresses and pillows from competition to competition, the team finally arrived in Beijing in August 2008 for its next Summer Games. It was the ultimate test of their 1% strategy. The result? They quadrupled their gold medal count, locking down a team record of eight gold medals in the Beijing games before maintaining that record number again during the hometown Olympic Games that followed in London in 2012.

THE MAGIC OF 1% MOMENTS…
WHEN YOU'RE NOT AN OLYMPIAN

I know what you may be thinking: "Cool story about some elite professional athletes, but my only experience with the Olympics is watching it from my couch in my sweats. No problem, and for the record, samesies. So let me tell you about Dawn.

I first met Dawn when I led a workshop on burnout and self-care for a Working Parents Employee Resource Group (ERG) at her social justice non-profit. A passionate advocate and mother of three, in the aftermath of George Floyd's murder, Dawn had never been busier at work. With her stress at an all-time high, she was eager to find new ways to handle her daily work-life juggle when she joined a women's leadership cohort program I was running.

Each cohort session had a different topic, and when we got to our session about goal-setting, I asked the group, "What do you *truly* want?"

Initially, it was crickets. For the women in the room, it had been years since they last stopped to consider what they *wanted*, not just what was *needed*. Worse, as they began to speak up, it was difficult to watch how hard they were all being on themselves—expressing how ashamed and disappointed they were in themselves that they hadn't already achieved their goals.

Goals are challenging by design. Otherwise, we'd call them "stuff I did last year." It's something I reminded them of, that I'll remind you of, and that I remind myself of constantly.

So, with cyclists and 1% moments on the brain, I asked them: what was something *small* they really wanted to do?

"If I could do anything," Dawn piped up, "it would be to run. It used to be the thing that kept me sane and, I know that it's probably the one thing I need most, but I just don't feel like it's even remotely physically possible with everything I have on my plate right now."

I asked Dawn, "What's the smallest thing you could say 'yes' to tomorrow to make this possible?"

Hmm, she thought for a moment, *I guess I could set my alarm earlier so that I can get up and run for fifteen minutes before the kids get up.*

Great, we were headed somewhere. "And what's the smallest thing you could say 'no' to in order to protect that commitment?" I asked back.

"Well, that's much easier—I will say no to hitting the Snooze button." She laughed for a moment before she corrected herself. "Wait, actually, that might be the hard part because it's just so tempting. I am really, *really* tired when my alarm goes off each morning."

"Great, let's make a plan: how could you say 'no' to that snooze button?"

"Okay, I'm going to ask my partner to literally push me out of the bed when it goes off."

The next day, Dawn posted in our cohort's private messaging group that she ran. It was just a ten-minute jog, but we all cheered her on and celebrated the fact that by jogging for just ten minutes a day, she was living a 1% moment for her goals.

Six months later, I sat down at my laptop on a cold December morning with a hot cup of coffee and saw I had an email from Dawn. Delighted to see her name in my inbox months after wrapping our cohort program, I opened it up to find a thank you note for a holiday gift I had sent to her:

> *Participating in your women's leadership group was a highlight of the year for me and I often find myself thinking back to things we discussed in those meetings. Work has been nuts… but one of my goals was to run more and I ended up running my first marathon in October!*

This busy working mom of three ran a *marathon* by starting with a single ten-minute jog. Like Brailsford said about his own team, it wasn't about perfection but progression. Dawn crossed the literal finish line to her goals, 1% at a time.

THE FOUR AVOIDING-OUR-GOALS TRAPS

The Old Playbook taught us that if we set a goal and didn't achieve it, we were a failure. That line of reasoning has created four distinct traps that I've seen high-achieving women fall into that keeps them *avoiding* their goals, rather than getting after them:

> **Avoiding-Our-Goals Trap #1: We get overwhelmed by the overwhelm itself.** We are so busy, and the goal seems like it will take *so much* effort that we stop ourselves from pursuing it because we get overwhelmed by the overwhelm itself.

So we distract ourselves from the overwhelm inside the "busy" of the to-do list items of the day, the big projects of the quarter, the family commitments, holiday or summer travel, and a never-ending list of things to distract ourselves with.

In the fleeting moments of quiet when we're taking the dog for a walk or washing our hair in the shower, the goal creeps back in. But it's so overwhelming that we say, "This is too much right now. I'll think about this later when I have time," and then we go back into that cycle of being busy.

Getting overwhelmed by the overwhelm itself is like saying you're going to start a diet tomorrow and then swinging through McDonald's for a Big Mac and a shake. It's not a plan. It's procrastination. Spoiler: we're going to dig even further into this in our chapter on *Reassessing Productivity & Reclaiming Time.*

> **Avoiding-Our-Goals Trap #2: "I just have to get through this..."** This all-too-common line of reasoning creates a passive form of career drift and goal

avoidance. We convince ourselves that our issue isn't with our *goals* but with *everything else* around us.

What's so insidious about this bad habit is that we think we're moving forward when we are really just experiencing career drift—letting our careers carry us instead of charting our own course toward our goals and priorities. It's like trying to count your steps on a fitness tracker while standing still on a moving walkway inside the airport. You might be moving forward, but you're not making progress.

Avoiding-Our-Goals Trap #3: We call our perfectionism "planning." One of the most dangerous stories we tell ourselves about our goals is that we can't talk about them or pursue them "until we have a plan." This story typically results in endless list-making, extensive research, and the creation of detailed five-year plans.

Goals are often stretchy, scary, and raw, which is what makes them both exciting and ripe opportunities for activating our perfectionistic bad habits. Perhaps what's most dangerous about this is when we mistake goal "planning" for goal "perfection," we feel like we're making progress, but we're really just making Google Docs. Worse, we're actually missing opportunities to share our half-baked ideas with people who can help us perfect the recipe (more on that later).

Avoiding-Our-Goals Trap #4: We negotiate against ourselves. What about when we're damn sure about what we want? That's where this last goal trap comes into play, when we start to negotiate against ourselves instead of going after it.

"Oh, I can't pursue that goal because it would require a pay cut, and I just can't afford it," or "I would really love to pursue this opportunity at work, but I'm afraid the additional travel will be impossible for my family."

As somebody who worked in sales for years, let me be clear: everything in life is negotiable, and the only person who loses when you bet against yourself is you.

Too often, we declare our goals "undoable" when, actually, we just need to get creative in designing around them. We negotiate against ourselves instead of sitting down and mapping out our needs and wants across the four core quadrants of our lives: professional, personal, family, and financial.

WHEN GOALS ARE HIDING IN PLAIN SIGHT

When Ronnie arrived at our first coaching session, she had a five-year plan: Year 1, get a new job. Year 2, thrive at the new job. Year 3, get pregnant and take maternity leave. Year 4, get the hang of working mom life. Year 5, pursue her real passion and open a clothing boutique.

She was a classic #3 on the Avoiding-Our-Goals Traps list, mislabeling her quest for perfection as "strategic planning." Ronnie thought she was in control because she had a plan—and, listen, I wasn't going to blow that plan up. At least not at our *very first* session.

I needed to learn more, and so did she. We jumped in together, and the first order of business was helping Ronnie navigate out of a toxic work environment. With her full focus on job searching, it took her less than ninety days to achieve her Year 1 goal.

As Ronnie settled into her new job, we could now move on to Ronnie's self-described "real passion"—her clothing business. She was a planner, so by the time Ronnie came to our coaching engagement, she had already made a business plan, designed a business name, and (again) created a very robust five-year plan.

I didn't understand—why did this have to wait five years?

We started digging and unsurprisingly found our usual suspect: the Inner Critic. There was all the textbook internal chatter about the risks of doing something new when she had just scored this dream job.

There was also the fact that Ronnie's mom had worked for *Vogue*. It didn't give her any connections for her nascent business but, instead, gave her a major perfectionism-and-external-validation complex about everything being "good enough."

She pushed on the need for a five-year plan, explaining, "Randi, this is a totally normal thing to do. I'm delaying gratification so that I will be more successful when I get it."

"No, you're not," I rebutted. "You're *denying* gratification. You have told me that clothing and fashion are your true passions in life, and you're not giving yourself permission to pursue them for half a decade."

After a long pause, all I got was, "Hmmm." Finally, she said, "You *might* be right. I don't *think* I am, but now I'm not sure."

So I asked her, "What's the smallest way you could pursue this passion that doesn't involve filing paperwork like getting your LLC, making lists, or doing research?"

Coincidentally, a friend texted her saying she had just gotten her bonus, and she wanted to treat herself to a new work bag. Ronnie agreed that she would take her friend shopping and play stylist for the day.

"Oh, and do me a fave?" I asked her just as our coaching call was coming to an end. "Will you take a bunch of pictures when you go?" Ronnie said sure but asked why. "Just trust me," I said before we ended the call.

When Ronnie came to our next coaching session, her energy was electric. She'd had a blast shopping with her friend and sent me a few of the pictures. As we debriefed the experience, it became clear to Ronnie that she already had a business:

> I realized I had been doing this all along. I did have a business: it wasn't a boutique business, but it was a styling business. This was already the content I was always sharing on Instagram—like my favorite makeup tips or an outfit I was loving—and I was always the friend somebody asked when they needed a new bag or the perfect dress for their rehearsal dinner.

The reason I asked her to snap pics on the shopping trip, I reminded her, was because she already had over 1,000 followers—something any new business owner would drool over. They were already used to tuning in to her posts, stories, and reels for tips on fashion. It wasn't brick-and-mortar, but it was hiding in plain sight all along.

"Of course…" Ronnie realized, "that's *exactly when* all the Inner Critic stuff came up about my mom working at *Vogue* and my not being good enough and about how my only 'true styling experience' was a summer working at J. Crew."

Reminding Ronnie that the Inner Critic just wants to be comforted, I challenged her to simply go back to the facts.

She made an inventory of all the things she was constantly being asked about. There were product recommendations like: What bronzer is best? There were event-specific styling questions like: What should I wear to my engagement party? Lastly were fashion trends like: Can petites wear nineties-style jeans? (FYI, according to Ronnie, the answer is yes, if you have them properly hemmed and styled.)

There were countless unknowns, and she had so many questions—from what types of content people would want to see to what she should charge. But those questions couldn't be answered inside a vacuum. So Ronnie started polling friends, pitching ideas like a closet makeover to people who engaged with her posts, and collecting data from the responses. At first, she was scared to put herself and her burgeoning business out there. She was much more comfortable with a spreadsheet analysis of pricing and service options.

It took her a single conversation with a former coworker—who asked to hire her *mid-chat*—for Ronnie to learn one simple thing: "There was literally no downside to experimenting. Originally, I thought there was, but I was wrong. Experimenting will tell you whether you're doing the right thing. When I started bringing my ideas in contact with my audience, I was like, 'Oh my god! I love this, and so do they!' I quickly realized that I was *meant* to do this."

It's how she also quickly learned her pricing was too low and about all the add-ons her clients were willing to pay for—things she would have never come up with by herself. After experimenting in earnest for a few months, she finally got up the courage to post on Instagram that she was officially open for business. She posted just as she went to dinner with her husband and left her phone in the car so she wouldn't compulsively check it the whole time they were in the restaurant. After getting through dinner as "a terrible, anxious mess," she came back to her phone and was blown away by the response.

Within a hundred days, she had stepped away from her five-year business plan and launched the business that was right underneath her. Like so many brilliant women, her goals were so much closer than she thought they were. They were hiding in plain sight.

Her advice to every other woman out there? "Give yourself permission and stop overthinking it. Start living your passions, not planning them."

WHEN YOUR GOALS ARE ITERATIVE...
NOT IMMACULATE

Unlike our super-planner Ronnie, when Kat Norton was locked down in her parents' home during the early days of the pandemic, she did not have a five-year plan or a specific goal in mind. She did, however, have her iPhone, her laptop, and a passion: "I just genuinely loved to teach Excel."

At the time, Kat was working for a global consulting firm doing securitization interviews for banks (like you, I'm not sure what that is, but it sounds pretty monotonous). In her free time at work, however, she built out an Excel training course to help teach her colleagues how they could improve their spreadsheet skills. The classes were a total hit.

Participants loved Kat's fun and *human* classes so much that when management got wind of them, they saw an opportunity. Soon, they began flying her around to the company's different offices to teach teams within the company.

When the COVID-19 pandemic arrived in March 2020, both Kat's frequent flier segments and her Excel training classes came to a screeching halt. Like many people in her twenties, she soon found herself hunkered down at her parents' home with "a *lot* more time on [her] hands."

If you're expecting me to tell you that this is also the exact moment when she did something with those Excel skills and her completely basic office equipment, this is where you'd be wrong.

A self-described "recovering shy kid and anxious adult," in early April 2020, Kat started to get curious about mindfulness. She began meditating, journaling, and for the first time, she recalls, taking time to get in touch with herself. She wasn't actively hiding out on any big goals, but she also wasn't racing to make huge leaps. She was just slowing down to listen to what was inside of her.

Then, seemingly out of nowhere, she turned to her mom one day and blurted, "Mom, I'm going to be rich and famous soon, so I need you to prepare your nervous system for that." Her mom laughed, assuming she was joking. This was her "shy kid"—who was locked down, to boot.

Kat wasn't joking, though. She had this gut feeling that she was onto something even though she wasn't sure what it was. Kat smiled and told her mom, "Just watch."

"And then I got this intuition to put Excel on TikTok," she told Nilay Patel on the *Decoder* podcast, explaining that it was so out of the blue that "I didn't even have a TikTok app on my phone at the time."

That's when Kat's Inner Critic and Intuition started to duke it out: "I had so much resistance to it because my mental voice was saying, 'You're twenty-seven years old. You cannot make a TikTok.' My gut voice was arguing, 'Make the TikTok.'"

Kat told her mom and her boyfriend, then climbed back up to her childhood room. She created a TikTok account as Miss Excel and made her first video—no professional equipment involved.

She started posting a video a day. On the fourth day, her video topped 100,000 views. After posting again on the fifth and sixth days, the CEO of an IT company sent her an email: "Hey, I love your teaching style. I'm looking to create training videos in G-Suite products for students, parents, and teachers." Could she help, he asked, as hundreds of thousands of schools around the country had just made the decision to move to virtual school for the remainder of the year?

She thought to herself, *I'm clearly a Microsoft gal, but I learn quickly. The spreadsheet products are similar.* So she responded with three words.

"Sure, I'm game."

And that's when she made her first capital expenditure: a ring light. Kat was stunned by her own success:

> *At this point, it's day six on TikTok, and I'm already making money. I decided that I'm just going to keep this thing rolling because I'm helping a lot of people—even though I wasn't really getting paid off the Miss Excel, social media part of the equation. Within three weeks I went viral on a whole other scale. I looked at my phone to see that one of my videos hit 3.6 million views. I had 100,000 followers on TikTok. At that point, I asked myself: now what do I do?*

Instead of getting mired in what she *should* be doing, Kat stayed curious about what was *possible* next. That attitude would prove to be prescient when rumors began swirling in June 2020 that TikTok might be shut down in the US, which risked shutting her whole business down with it.

As an insurance policy, Kat created a Miss Excel Instagram account but noticed that only 2,000 people migrated over with her to the new platform. Still, she didn't get distressed. She got creative and started playing with one of Instagram's new features: reels, which unbeknownst to her, were being weighted more heavily by the app's behind-the-scenes algorithms.

She went viral *again*—no fancy social media consultants, no video editors, no market research, no customer acquisition plan, and no ad spend. Just her ideas, her passion, and her posting Excel tips in fun Instagram reels. All while still working at her full-time job, she built a six-figure business in six months during the spare hours she had on nights and weekends.

When she scored her first big press interview from *Morning Brew* in October 2020, she got a tip from a great business coach: she should be able to pitch a product in the interview. So she took a few weeks of PTO from the consulting firm and built out her first Excel course with a plan to launch it on Black Friday. Once again, it was a smash success. Less than sixty days later, she was making more money from the course *alone* than from her consulting firm salary, benefits, and healthcare insurance combined. The path was clear: she quit her day job, taking Miss Excel full-time so she could develop more courses and subscription packages.

With most of her income passive from on-demand classes and subscription packages, by April 2021, she had her first six-figure month. The growth didn't stop, and by November 2021, she had her first six-figure day.

Her incredible success didn't start with some premeditated grand plan. It started with an idea, followed by another idea, and another—coupled with curiosity and a willingness to put herself out there.

At the time of publication, Kat still runs the now multi-million-dollar business by herself: no staff except for a virtual assistant who helps her with some scheduling and emails. Ironically, aside from her accounting, she doesn't even use Excel to track her own business goals: "I still go based off my intuition... I still do me, and that authenticity is what really drives it."

THE NEW PLAYBOOK FOR
GETTING AFTER YOUR GOALS

Yes, goals are hard, stretchy, overwhelming, and scary at times. But if you've picked up anything from Dawn, Ronnie, or Kat (a.k.a. Miss Excel), you've also probably realized by now they can be remarkably doable when we break them down.

That's why as we write the New Playbook for designing your goals, I'm dying for you to chuck out that Old Playbook story—the one where we need to write our goals in stone, and we're a failure if we don't achieve them. As we've discussed, that keeps too many of us from getting started on our own personal marathons (like Dawn) and career pivots (like Ronnie and Kat). Instead, here are five tools for getting after your goals.

#1. **Start with a Simple List.** One thing that consistently stuns me is how *infrequently* the driven women I work with pause to consider what they actually want. We're so quick to prioritize everyone else's needs— our team, our boss, our family, our friends—before our own and to focus (or obsess) over where we can improve our productivity and input.

To stay clear of being overwhelmed by the overwhelm itself (Avoiding-Our-Goals Trap #1), I recommend simply breaking your goals down into four categories. Pro tip: you can also try "desires" or "wishes" on for size if "goals" intimidates you.

These can be as big as "scoring my dream job" or as small as "get outside more." You always have permission to edit so, as you jot your wish list down, think of the chart below as more of an experimental whiteboard than a codified strategic plan. You can also download a printable copy of this chart at www.somethingmajorcoaching.com/book.

Personal	Professional
Family/Relationships	Financial

Note that "personal" is intentionally separate from "family/relationships" and that "financial" has been carved out from "professional"—even though they're inherently related.

In order to stay clear of negotiating against ourselves (Avoiding-Our-Goals Trap #4), we want to simply get it all down on paper, segmenting out the different facets of our desires, so we can make a thoughtful plan for how to integrate them.

Remember what the late Supreme Court Justice Ruth Bader Ginsburg famously said when asked how she "did it all" over the course of her career: "You can't have it all, all at once. Who—man or woman—has it all, all at once? Over my lifespan I think I have had it all. But in different periods of time, things were rough."

> **#2. Make Like an Olympian with 1% Moves.** I don't care if you ever ride a bicycle, do a fancy gymnastics routine, or do any kind of super-fancy-spinny-divey thing into the water. If you have gotten this far, you are an Olympian, and your sport is your life goals. You do not need to hire a surgeon to teach you hand washing or experiment with wind tunnels to carve out your own 1% moments. Remember, Dawn started by setting her alarm to run *one* morning and ran a marathon just months later.

I can't encourage you enough to "go small" in order to go big. It's how we sidestep being overwhelmed by the overwhelm itself (Avoiding-Our-Goals Trap #1), getting trapped inside of "I just need to get through this" (Avoiding-Our-Goals Trap #2) and mistaking our perfectionism for "planning" (Avoiding-Our-Goals Trap #3). Here are some questions to help you get started on designing your 1% moments.

- What's the smallest thing I can *say yes* to today to advance my goal?

- What's the smallest thing I can *say no* to today to advance my goal?
- If I carve out two hours on the weekend, what progress can I make toward my goals on a Sunday afternoon?
- Who is one person I can talk to about my goal? Even in its messiest or most nascent form?
- Who knows something about my goals, and what can I learn from them?

Remember: there is nothing that will get you to your big goals faster than making small moves. Your 1% moves matter, so treat them like they count.

#3. Consider Your Goals a Contact Sport. The fastest way to discover or achieve your goals is to get out of the Google Doc and into conversation with other people. Every woman in this chapter leaned on other people to achieve her goals—and they did so while their ideas were total pipe dreams or musings.

Dawn asked her partner to make sure she didn't hit snooze for that first ten-minute run. Miss Excel told her mom she was posting her first video, and Ronnie asked potential customers questions instead of just pitching them services.

It's tempting to stay quiet about our goals when they're new, big, or scary. We don't want to be judged or waste people's time until we have it more thought out. But that's exactly why we want to put our goals in contact with other people while they're still half-baked—sometimes they have the question, idea, or introduction that is the missing ingredient we've needed to refine our recipe all along.

Trust me, I know how hard this is. Do you remember Claire Wasserman of Ladies Get Paid who we heard from in our *Ditching Perfectionism* and *Untethering From External Validation* chapters?

The summer before I wrote this book, I was sitting in a restaurant with her in Los Angeles and brought my copy of her book, *Ladies Get Paid*, for her to sign. As she was writing "LOVE YOU," the final words of her inscription on the cover page, she looked up and asked me when I'd write my book. It was a dream, but it always felt so out of reach. I told her about it without the pressure to have all the answers. Instead, I started asking her questions.

Less than a year later, I'd interview her for my book, and today, you are reading these words in your very own hands. Yes, I wrote the book myself—but that lunch with Claire was one of the many mentoring and ideation conversations along the way that made it feel 1% more possible and ultimately made it happen. Our goals are a contact sport. Get off the bench and get out there to find out who is on your team.

#4. Treat Your Goals like a Fine Wine, Not a Kegger.

We live in a world of messages like "go hard or go home," and that can be intimidating when it comes to our goals. That's why I want you to treat your goals more like a fine wine than a kegger. Too often, when we identify a goal, we run hard at it. That can be awesome, but sometimes it can be the equivalent of doing a keg stand. It seems really exciting, and you get a rush… but the next day, you wake up with a massive hangover and bloated belly, wondering why you even thought you liked beer in the first place.

Instead, I want you to treat your goals like a fine wine—sipping and savoring, instead of chugging. We've talked about the "sipping" piece, focusing on small 1% moments, but "savoring" is just as important. Our goals are often a long-game. It's critical to celebrate the small wins when they happen. This is something Ronnie did as she leaned into making them a contact sport. She celebrated every DM, every time a post got tons of likes, and every time she learned something from her future client base.

Celebrating the wins is what will sustain you in going after big goals (especially the ones that take lots of time to achieve). Plus, it'll just make life more fun in the process. As somebody who annually sends her clients custom champagne bottles, I can tell you that wine is not required, but it is welcomed.

#5. Remember, You Already Have a Toolkit. By now, you have so many tools (we still have more to come), so don't be afraid to use them. Below is a cheat sheet on how the tools you've already developed inside the New Playbook can support you in getting after your goals.

- **Ditching Perfectionism:** Nobody's path to their goals is picture perfect—no matter what they try to show you on Instagram or LinkedIn. Consider where you might be falling into old traps and bad habits when it comes to your perfectionism. What "Good Girl" habits are holding you back? What do you believe about failure being anything less than perfection? Where are you exhausting yourself by trying to overachieve instead of trying your best?

- **Quieting Your Inner Critic:** Instead of being paralyzed by your self-doubt, get to work decoding it. What does your Inner Critic believe, and what are at least two other scenarios that could pan out here which would make that voice's prediction about this goal wrong? What does your Inner Critic believe, and what can you trust (or not trust) about that?

- **Reclaiming Intuition:** Like Miss Excel said, the key is that she still goes based off her intuition, not the data—even though she is *literally* the Excel data maven. So how could you slow down and use the intuition tools we covered? As Sara Blakely would ask you if you were her Spanx employee: what do the dots *between* the data say? Your intuition holds a profound amount of intelligence around your goals— if you give yourself permission to access it.

Doing big things is about making lots of small moves. Clinical psychologist and author Dr. Meg Jay reminds us that our daily choices are like boarding a westbound flight at LAX: "Right after takeoff, a slight change in course is the difference between landing in Alaska or Fiji." As we'll cover in the next chapter, we also have the ability to chart our own course when we land somewhere completely unexpected.

CHAPTER 6:

REBOUNDING WHEN THE PLAN BLOWS UP

———

When it comes to life, sometimes we swipe right, but the universe (or just a single bad actor) swipes left.

That was certainly the case for Whitney Wolfe Herd. At just twenty-two, Wolfe Herd left the job she took after college at a company called Cardify—an app, which allowed customers to either swipe left or swipe right on digital loyalty cards—taking a flier on a new idea. She joined the founding crew of innovators who catalyzed a swipe-right-for-yes and swipe-left-for-no revolution with their hookup app (ahem, I mean "dating" app). Perhaps you've heard of it? It's called Tinder.

While growth at Tinder was hot, her romantic relationship with one of Tinder's co-founders went on ice. When Wolfe Herd swiped left on their relationship, he tried to swipe left on her career.

As *Time* magazine reported, Wolfe Herd was allegedly subjected to verbal abuse (being told to "shut up" in meetings), physical abuse (being spat at in the face at an office party), emotional abuse (relegated to "fetching breakfast" as Tinder's vice president of marketing), and—*yup, I know you could guess what was coming next*—sexual harassment. Wolfe Herd was even allegedly called a "whore" in a meeting and sexually objectified in others that she didn't attend—reportedly having her breast size debated and discussed.

Even after filing a sexual harassment suit against Tinder in 2014, the abuse didn't stop. The arena simply changed—and got bigger—as her trauma played out in public. The workplace abuse and online onslaught that followed were crushing. But it was in one of those enough-is-enough moments that Wolfe Herd's next venture, Bumble, was born. While Wolfe Herd's relationship and job had been blown up, her *raison d'être* had not.

So, Wolfe Herd lit her own dynamite in the world of dating apps: "Scarred by the online harassment she endured after the Tinder blow up, Wolfe Herd wanted to make an app where women could give each other compliments," explains *Time* reporter, Charlotte Alter, who has reported on Wolfe Herd's story for years, interviewing the tech titan for the better part of the decade.

Wolfe Herd was driven by the need to create a safer space for women online: "Honestly," she told Alter years later on the eve of Bumble's eventual IPO, "my ambition comes from abusive relationships. I've never had this healthy male relationship until I created it. I engineered an ecosystem of healthy male relationships in my life."

In 2014, Wolfe Herd launched Bumble in earnest, designing it as the first dating app where women were in control. But Wolfe Herd wasn't a programmer. As a co-founder at Tinder, she was the brains behind the app's marketing and branding.

Setting up shop in Austin, Texas, Wolfe Herd hired her first employee: her sorority sister from Southern Methodist

University, Caroline Ellis Roche. The duo wasted no time building buzz as the Bumble app was under development.

Using a two-bedroom apartment in Austin as their HQ, they stored branded Bumble merchandise in a bathtub. On weekends, they pounded the pavement, handing out T-shirts, balloons, and even Hanky-Panky brand thong underwear in Bumble's signature yellow across college campuses in Texas.

"We started marketing Bumble before we had any sort of product," Roche recalled to *Time* in 2021, "and Whitney always said, 'It's a lifestyle brand, it's a lifestyle brand, it's a lifestyle brand.' That's what we leaned into."

To be clear, women didn't just love the free swag; they loved the experience on the app. Unlike every other traditional dating app on the market, on Bumble only women could make the first move and initiate a conversation with a man they were interested in (for LGBTQ+ matches, messages could flow in either direction). This prevented men from bombarding women users with unwanted advances and messages. It was, perhaps, the one place on the internet where women were in control.

Women loved it, and men signed up *because* women loved it—a virtuous cycle that exploded Bumble's growth right out of the gate. Within the first six months of its launch, the app boasted approximately a half million users who were sending nearly a quarter-million messages per day. Wolfe Herd quickly snagged seed funding from the sought-after European tech investor Andrey Andreev and built out a six person team (five of whom were women—practically unheard of anywhere else in tech).

With an unrelenting focus on its unique user experience, Bumble's growth continued to swell: acquiring new users at a drool-worthy, week-after-week clip of 15 percent in the early days and ultimately boasting twelve million users by the time Wolfe Herd took the company public on February 11, 2021.

When she listed Bumble on the NASDAQ with a record-breaking offering, Wolfe Herd—at only thirty-one years old—became the youngest woman to ever take a company public. Within the first two hours of trading, she also became one of the youngest female billionaires on the planet, courtesy of Bumble's skyrocketing share price.

There was no doubt about it: while it felt like life had swiped left when she left Tinder, she had swiped right. When her plan had a blow-up, she transformed it into the ultimate glow-up.

SWIPING RIGHT ON LIFE (NOT TINDER)

Sometimes the plan just blows up.

While most of us cannot relate to being billionaires, many of us can relate to the fear and vulnerability Wolfe Herd experienced when our plans explode around something we care about deeply like our career, our reputation, or a relationship.

While it's tempting to sit with the Inner Critic as they roll the tape and play Monday morning quarterback—"you *should* have known better; you *should* have made better choices"—that does not help us move forward. It only holds us back.

Let's remember that when something "blows up," it is inherently disruptive and destructive to our lives. That's why the key is to focus on our rebuilding plan.

Our Inner Critics are much better at punishing us for the mess than problem-solving the clean-up strategy. While understanding lessons can move us forward, too often we move beyond healthy levels of accountability and understanding. We move into the self-destructive territory of self-flagellation—and that's *not* helpful.

Mostly because, as leadership expert Marcus Buckingham reminds us, we cannot remediate our way to excellence. On the contrary, as the late Nelson Mandela said, "The greatest glory in living lies not in never failing, but in rising every time we fall." Adding separately, "I never lose. I either win or I learn."

That's why the key to moving forward when the plan has blown up is not to swipe left to a plan focused on remediation and self-discipline. Instead, swipe right on a plan based on optimization and self-love. Consider the difference:

Remediation & Self-Discipline	Optimization & Self-Love
Makes decisions based on fear of failure	Grants permission to make mistakes and learn
Focuses on "fixing" what is broken or missing	Invests time and energy in strengths; utilizes existing resources
Makes decisions from a place of "should"	Makes decisions from a place of "could"
Prioritizes what others expect, think, or need when making decisions	Prioritizes own expectations, thoughts, or need when making decisions
Works harder	Works smarter
Perseverates over nightmare scenarios	Is unafraid to pursue dreams

Embracing a perspective of optimization and self-love simply moves us forward. This isn't "feel-good" stuff; this is actually the hardest stuff of all. When we're buried in the rubble of self-doubt or shame after the plan has blown up, it's actually harder to swipe right. But it's also incredibly important. To quote Ruth Bader Ginsburg again, "So often in life, the things that you regard as an impediment turn out to be great, good fortune."

Ginsburg was right: when the plan blows up, it can move us forward, even when that moving forward is in unexpected or tender ways. We consistently go further when we optimize instead of remediate, when we lean into the things we most trust and treasure about ourselves instead of obsessing over the things we don't.

WHEN WE *THINK* THE PLAN HAS BLOWN UP

Risa always wanted to be a doctor. After years (and years) of school, exams, residency, and fellowship, she was living her dream. Just like every person can tell you the story about how they met their partner, every physician can tell you how they met their specialty.

Moved by the stories of the doctors who were on the front lines of New York's HIV/AIDS epidemic—and the mind-bending complexity of treating new and unknown diseases—Risa fell head over heels with infectious disease. She knew she wanted to be there on the frontlines when the next epidemic hit.

But when the first COVID-19 case was confirmed in New York City on March 1, 2020, Risa knew her plans were toast. Like the shot heard around the world, the confirmation of that first case in New York seemingly fired up every gal-pal group text in America, including one between me, Risa, and our other two high school friends, Brittany and Danielle.

An infectious disease physician at New York's Mt. Sinai Hospital, Risa—oops, pardon me, I meant Dr. Risa Fuller—was nine months pregnant. Like most first-time moms, Risa was nervous about giving birth. But, as she followed the news, Risa started to get scared.

Lovingly known in our group for how level-headed, unflappable, and un-touchy-feely she is (seriously, *do not* try to hug her), Risa was, in her own words, "totally freaking out." She and her colleagues were watching cases as they were confirmed in other parts of the world and country, just waiting for the other shoe to drop.

"A few days before [I gave birth], I was still seeing infectious disease cases at Mt. Sinai Hospital," she recalls. "We suspected COVID-19 cases and, at thirty-nine weeks pregnant, I was treating patients in the hospital who had all the symptoms of the virus. Without testing, we didn't have any documented patients yet—but we all knew it was there."

A few days later, on Sunday, March 1st, state officials announced the first confirmed case in New York City and Risa went into labor. It was a disaster.

According to the girl whom I have never once seen cry in decades of friendship, even amidst breakups and board exams, "I cried throughout the entire labor." After laboring and pushing for hours, Risa had an emergency C-section: "My glasses were so dirty from the tears that the anesthesiologist asked me if he could wipe them, which only made me cry harder." The floodgates literally opened—sobbing through the birth and into the recovery room, she cried so much, "that I was literally dehydrated."

With her new daughter Aria in one arm and an IV bag of fluids in the other, her mind raced: "All I could think is, *I have to get her out. I don't want her in the hospital when this thing blows up.*"

Fueled by a stress cocktail of her maternal instincts, deep knowledge of infectious disease, and the swirl of postpartum hormones, she tried as hard as she could to get home to her apartment on Manhattan's Upper West Side—something she concedes in retrospect, "is not easy when you're recovering from a major abdominal surgery."

Then, as soon as Risa was home, she yearned to be back at work. While most of us took our laptops home from work and started to learn the full functionality of Zoom in those early weeks, Risa was at home when all of her colleagues were in overdrive at the hospital.

The result was a crushing mix of first-time-mom-stress and total professional FOMO: "I was reading *New England Journal of Medicine* articles at 3 a.m. while nursing, scrolling all these physician Facebook groups in the middle of the night, and watching the news all day. The amount of stress and anxiety I was feeling at that moment was insane."

Twenty-one days after Aria was born, Risa's husband Bill received an email from work. Cases were surging in New York City, and the note explained that Columbia University's Irving Medical Center needed all hands on deck. Bill—pardon me again; that's Dr. William Fuller, who practices as a primary care physician and teaches on Columbia's faculty—was shifting from telemedicine to an emergency rotation.

Sure, every family that adds a baby has to figure out their own way to juggle everything. But this was extreme. Between the schedule needed at work and the quarantines required to keep Risa and Aria safe, it looked like Bill would have to move out for months.

That was not going to fly, so Bill got creative and went to work trading shifts with his colleagues at Columbia. Instead of spreading out each two-week rotation with a mix of day shifts, night shifts, and days off, he'd do a week of seven consecutive nights, followed immediately by a week of seven consecutive days. After working fourteen days and nights straight, he'd then get two consecutive weeks off which would allow him to quarantine and travel to Risa—who moved thirty miles away to her parents' home on Long Island the first day Bill went to the COVID ward.

While Bill captured the peaks and valleys of those early COVID-19 nights in a raw and moving daily video diary, Risa's days felt endless and monotonous. She was stuck sitting on the sidelines for what she considered a "career-defining moment," grieving her chance to be on the front lines, to make a difference:

> Before the pandemic, the older Infectious Disease doctors always talked about AIDS—what it was like during the outbreak and why they went into Infectious Disease because of it. I always wondered about what might be the new disease for me when I chose this specialty, and here I was at home... just watching it happen.

> I had such mixed feelings: guilty that I'm not helping, relief that I'm not out there because I have this baby, and also kind of jealous that I'm missing out on this major thing. This thing that is what all the Infectious Disease doctors are going to talk about for decades—and I'm going to be at the conferences for the rest of my career saying, 'Oh yeah, I was out on maternity leave.'

So Risa cried. But in between diaper changes and feeds, she kept reading journal articles, staying active in text chains and Facebook groups with colleagues, and soaking up everything she could about COVID-19. Tapping back into her purpose and passion, she resolved she would make up for lost time.

She could not move backward, but she had a choice about how she moved forward. So twelve weeks after Aria was born, and twelve weeks plus one day after the first coronavirus case was confirmed in New York, Risa returned to work.

Normal concerns about childcare and pumping accommodations were replaced by concerns about quarantines and access to PPE (personal protective equipment)—but Risa thrived. In retrospect, it feels like she never missed a beat.

Of course, one of the hardest things to do when our goals and plans blow up is have perspective, something Risa developed. Now a mom of two, her son Nathan was born just as the Omicron surge swept the country and she thinks about how her maternity leave is a different kind of legacy.

"Randi, you know that story about how you used to go around as a little kid telling people, 'my name is Randi, and I'm a natural beauty' because your aunt told you so when you were a little kid?" Risa asked me as I was interviewing her about this—and, yes, this is indeed a true story that I am only telling you because it's so integral to Risa's point. She then clarified, "I want Aria to go around telling people, 'My mommy is an Infectious Disease doctor, and I was a pandemic baby.' I want her to be proud of what we did and her small part in the story."

When I asked Risa if she had any other advice for women on what to do when the plan blows up, she paused and said, "Yes, I do have one more thing to say." I leaned in with my pen in my hand, and Risa asked, "Can you please make sure that 'natural beauty' story makes it in? Because that is one of my favorite things ever."

Embarrassing childhood stories aside, Risa reminds us that sometimes we *think* the plan is in shambles when we're really experiencing an unexpected moment as the bigger plan unfolds.

WHEN WE CHOOSE TO BLOW UP THE PLAN

It was just after two in the morning when Steven Johnson walked into the East Village bar where Robin Arzón, a rising senior at NYU, was having drinks with a few of her friends. Armed with three guns, kerosene, and a sword that was nearly three feet long, Johnson took the bar hostage and held Arzón at gunpoint after dousing her in kerosene.

"And this is kind of when time slows down," Arzón recalled in 2002 to *The New York Times*. "I became a pseudo-negotiator with the NYPD."

A few hours into their standoff, while Johnson was still holding a gasoline-doused Arzón by the hair, two other patrons at the bar tried to subdue him by attacking him from behind. A struggle ensued, Johnson began to shoot, and the NYPD stormed the bar. Three were wounded, but Arzón was not one of them. Miraculously escaping unharmed during the struggle, she was traumatized and turned to running as a form of healing.

Arzón continued running at Villanova Law, where she began racing in 10ks, but after law school life got busier. As a Litigation Associate at the New York office of Paul Hastings—one of the toniest law firms in the world—Arzón's hours were long. Under the crush of billable hours requirements and a seemingly never-ending pile of client matters, running became the ultimate luxury: "I would count down working eighty hours a week to the twenty minutes I could go for a run in Central Park."

Those twenty minutes were everything to her, and, with every run, she was getting more curious about the choices she was making with her life: "I thought, *That doesn't make any sense. I'm literally living for the seventy minutes a week I get to myself.* So what I started doing was, little by little, reclaiming some of my time back."

Arzón always thought she was going to be a career attorney but started to wonder, "There has to be a way to monetize this passion." Curious about how she could turn her love of fitness into a living, she "started with a ten-minutes-a-day rule that was blocked on my calendar that my team and my assistant knew was protected."

In those ten minutes, Arzón might send an email asking somebody in the fitness industry for an informational chat or just search Google to see whom she could email tomorrow: "Those ten minutes over two years actually amounted to quite a bit of time. That was how I took a little bit of my agency back."

Ten minutes at a time is how, as a rising Eighth-Year Associate, within spitting distance of that coveted Partner prize, Arzón blew up the plan—but blowing up the plan was not easy. First, there was the pressure and guilt she felt: "Coming from an [industry] where there weren't tons of Latinas, I felt like: Oh gosh, if I'm literally the [only] one at the law firm, how do I leave?" But Arzón knew this was her path and her passion.

Next, there was the practical element: "I was just trying to figure out how to pay my rent while running." Arzón couldn't see the grand plan, but she was truly, madly, deeply in love with movement, and trusted that following her passion would lead her in the right direction.

Staying curious about options and just trying to get through her next rent payment is how she discovered cycling: "When I left law, running was definitely my first love. I started teaching cycling classes honestly as a hobby. I was just like: You know what? I love this. I love doing it for my own fitness, so I just wanted to learn the bells and whistles on the science behind it."

Arzón got her first gig teaching spin at a tiny local studio in New York's Union Square—not too far, in fact, from the bar where Johnson once doused her in kerosene and held her at gunpoint. It wasn't glamorous. In fact, it was awkward: "When I was starting to learn how to teach spin, I couldn't order songs, I couldn't hear the beat, I couldn't speak while cycling… I mean there were classes where literally one person would show up."

But Arzón chalked it all up to a learning experience. In retrospect, she believes those awkward classes are what made her who she is today. Now, she says, "I'm so grateful for that experience: not only for the team who really helped form… my basis of my teaching, but even more so, all the times I failed in that studio."

It had been about six months since Arzón left Paul Hastings when she read an article about a company called Peloton in *Fast Company*, and she was taken by the model. Unlike most other boutique fitness experiences, which could only be experienced in-studio (like rival Soul Cycle), Peloton was early to the at-home-experience party. Arzón thought it was brilliant. "I realized this was the marriage of movement and modernity," she recalled to *Fortune*, years later.

So she opened her laptop: "I wrote an email to John Foley, the founder and CEO of Peloton, and said, 'I need to be working with you.'" She had a job two days later.

Beginning as an instructor, she was promoted to Vice President of Fitness Programming after only two years. Under Arzón's leadership, the brand grew steadily, opening additional studios in both New York and London, acquiring top talent, developing a Peloton treadmill, and expanding to mat-based fitness classes. Arzón was wildly successful, and at the company's peak, *CNBC* reported that Peloton membership swelled to three million paid subscribers.

Arzón blew up the plan to pursue her passions. Today, as a fitness celebrity, an executive, an ultra-marathoner, and a *New York Times* best-selling author, she wouldn't have it any other way—neither would millions of her devoted fans.

THE NEW PLAYBOOK FOR REBOUNDING WHEN THE PLAN BLOWS UP

As we've discussed, when the plan blows up, it is destructive and disruptive by design.

Let me be unequivocal: you have permission to have all the feels—just like Wolfe Herd did when she was getting trolled on the internet, like Risa did when she wondered if she was going to be changing diapers instead of being on the front lines for the most formative opportunity in her entire career, or like Arzón did when she was wondering how she'd pay rent.

So, yes, be with your feelings and also know that when the plan blows up, you have the mandate to reassess your priorities, reclaim your agency, and redesign your life. Here are five tools to rely on when this happens.

#1. Don't Mistake an Identity Crisis for Identity Foreclosure. Listen, if the plan blows up and you *don't* reckon with who you are and what your life is all about, then you either (1) have not processed that the plan has blown up or (2) have not actually experienced a true blow up.

In order to rebound, it's critical to stay focused on what is possible next. But many of us are quick to do just the opposite—closing ourselves off from the options and clinging to tunnel vision as we experience a psychological phenomenon known as "identity foreclosure."

It's the thing we experience when we're let go from that job and say, "But my career is my life!" or "It's too late to start something new." As more formally defined by the American Psychological Association, identity foreclosure is "a premature commitment to an identity ... [in which] the individual's commitment to the foreclosed identity occurs without exploring its value."

In his *New York Times* best-seller *Think Again*, psychologist Dr. Adam Grant explains how damaging this can be when we experience it in our work lives: "Identity foreclosure can stop us from evolving. In some ways, identity foreclosure is the opposite of an identity crisis. Instead of accepting uncertainty about who we want to become, we develop compensatory conviction and plunge head over heels into a career path."

You know you might be in identity foreclosure territory if you hear statements like these:

- "Well, that's the way it always is."
- "It's too late to change anything now."
- "That chance is long gone."
- "I'll never have an opportunity to do anything new/better/different again."

- "I missed the boat on going to grad school/trying that out/pursuing that passion."

Staying open about the possibilities doesn't just make us feel better; it helps us problem-solve more effectively. Harvard Business School professor Dr. Francesca Gino explains that curiosity is key: "When our curiosity is triggered, we think more deeply and rationally about decisions and come up with more creative solutions."

#2. Swipe Right on Optimization and Self-Love. As discussed, while our Inner Critics will want us to simply keep disciplining ourselves, if we want to move forward and move on, it is absolutely critical to adopt a perspective of Optimization and Self-Love. Consider the chart we looked at earlier in this chapter again:

Remediation & Self-Discipline	Optimization & Self-Love
Makes decisions based on fear of failure	Grants permission to make mistakes and learn
Focuses on "fixing" what is broken or missing	Invests time and energy in strengths; utilizes existing resources
Makes decisions from a place of "should"	Makes decisions from a place of "could"
Prioritizes what others expect, think, or need when making decisions	Prioritizes own expectations, thoughts, or need when making decisions
Works harder	Works smarter
Perseverates over nightmare scenarios	Is unafraid to pursue dreams

Now you tell me which feels like the better place to hang out if you want to make moves that matter. Thought so... but it can also be hard, so consider the following questions to help when "swiping right" on optimization and self-love:

- What is the smallest thing I know I can trust about myself?
- What is one strength I possess, and how can I use it here?
- What have I learned?
- When is another time when I have rebounded from a mistake or the unexpected?
- What's one thing I can do today to take a step forward?

Whitney Wolfe Herd modeled this when she started Bumble. She had been Tinder's marketing leader and, while she could not write code to develop the app that would make her a billionaire, she knew one thing: branding. Designing Bumble from the get-go as a "lifestyle brand," it was Wolfe Herd's savvy marketing that catapulted its launch.

Your Inner Critic will want to keep you focused on watching the replay: assessing what went wrong, perseverating over the moves you did or did not make, and obsessing over all the things you need to change about yourself. It will not move you forward. Only your strengths will move you forward—and you cannot access them if you are remediating your weaknesses and disciplining yourself for your (perceived) shortcomings.

#3. Get Gritty. Sometimes, the plan blows up around something we're not ready to let go of. One of the most important things we can do when that happens is to get gritty.

As grit guru and psychologist Dr. Angela Duckworth describes in the TED Talk that put both her and grit on the map, "Grit is passion and perseverance for very long-term goals. Grit is having stamina. Grit is sticking with your future, day in, day out, not just for the week, not just for the month, but for years, and working really hard to make that future a reality. Grit is living life like it's a marathon, not a sprint."

This was something Risa lived into. Yes, she was initially reeling (once again, please see "permission to feel all the feels" when the plan blows up), but she also bet on her future, her passion, and herself. In between midnight feedings and diaper changes, she was soaking up every ounce of medical literature and (credible) news she could find about COVID-19.

She was terrified about missing a "career-defining" moment, but, to Duckworth's point, she had the perspective to zoom out—she remembered her career *was* a marathon, not a sprint, and focused on training appropriately. It was her grit that drove her to make up for lost time when she got back in the game doing what she cared about most: helping people.

#4. **Lean Into 1% Moments.** When the plan has blown up (or you're jonesing to blow it up yourself), it's tempting to look for a grand gesture to get you where you want to go. Most of the time, however, there is no quick fix. As we learned from our Olympic-gold-medal-winning British cyclists in the last chapter, it's more effective to design a series of 1% moves than to look for a single, giant leap forward.

Arzón told *Fortune* in 2020, her decision to blow up the plan of being a career attorney was "a two-year process of figuring it out, doing informational interviews and thinking about it. We tend to think of the *Jerry Maguire* moment where you throw the books on the floor and everything changes. But our journeys don't work like that."

From carving out the time for a ten-minute informational interview to sending the cold email that would change her life to Peloton founder John Foley, Arzón's story is an incredible reminder of the power of 1% moments. So when the plan blows up, come back to these questions from our *Getting After Your Goals* chapter to design your own plan:

- What's the smallest thing I can *say yes* to today to move forward from here?
- What's the smallest thing I can *say no* to today to move forward from here?
- Who is one person I can talk to about this? Even in its messiest or most nascent form?
- Who might have a valuable perspective on my situation, and what can I learn from them?

#5. Choose Courage, Not Fearlessness. When the plan blows up, the elephant in the room is fear—and that's exactly why I want you to choose courage, not fearlessness, to face it. If you're like me, you grew up in or around "girl power" culture. We had posters, we had the Spice Girls, and we had a core message that we heard again and again: *Be fearless!* It set an impossibly high standard for us and, decades later, we're playing the price. That's because we rarely get the luxury of being "fearless" about anything—especially when the plan has blown up, and we're scared out of our minds.

Instead of fearlessness, I challenge you to choose courage. While both are modern-day synonyms of the word brave, we shouldn't use them interchangeably, and here's why: the root for courage is *cor*, Latin for heart. That's why, for years, to "act courageously" meant to act *from your heart* in the face of fear—not waiting it out until you were totally fearless. Courage allows us the space to feel fear *and* trust ourselves enough to move through it.

As Nelson Mandela once reflected, "I learned that courage was not the absence of fear, but the triumph over it. The brave man is not he who does not feel afraid but he who conquers that fear." Courage allows us to be *with* fear instead of mired in it.

Holocaust survivor and psychologist Viktor Frankl explains in his seminal work, *Man's Search for Meaning*, "The meaning of life always changes, but it never ceases to be... For what then matters is to bear witness to the uniquely human potential at its best, which is to transform a personal tragedy into a triumph, to turn one's predicament into a human achievement."

Written after the manuscript for his groundbreaking treatise on logotherapy (a school of psychology that he pioneered) was confiscated by the Nazis and destroyed upon his arrival at the Auschwitz concentration camp, Frankl's sentiments are a reminder that we can survive—and flourish—after even the greatest adversity.

For most of us, it is not a question of "if" the plan will blow up but "when" the plan will blow up and how we will react to it when it does. It is so critical to swipe right on

Optimization & Self-Love when it does. That is the only way to move forward, make progress, and find your next great adventure.

Every woman in this chapter who saw her plan blow up—Whitney Wolfe Herd, Dr. Risa Fuller, and Robin Arzón—came out bolder. I hope you will too.

CHAPTER 7:

OWNING YOUR MESSAGE

———

Ugh, is this too bitchy? Sophia thought as she sat watching the cursor blink inside the email pane.

The document she needed was already twenty minutes late. "Okay, this really needs to get moving," she thought. So she typed out a few new sentences and then furiously hit the delete button—*click, click, click, click, click*—ugh, that was too abrasive.

But this was time-sensitive. Now the document was *twenty-five* minutes late, and she hadn't even sent the damn email. She typed out a few words again and then slammed that delete button again—*click, click, click, click, click.* Ugh, but now it was too warm, and it didn't convey the urgency she needed.

She was a top performer at her firm, shepherding a major deal for her client, and she was wasting precious time writing (and rewriting) emails to a junior associate about a document that he was already late in returning.

This was a simple email, so why did it feel so hard?

THE HICCUP TEST

Whether it's writing a simple email or sharing a major win, owning our message at work can be extremely difficult. Even—and especially—for high-performing women. That was certainly the case for Lina.

For over a year, Lina and her team had been preparing for the world premiere of a new initiative in March 2020. That plan was upended overnight when Lina went home from work one day and just never went back.

As the hundred-year-old organization struggled to pivot to the new realities of remote-work life and transition their splashy in-person campaign launch to a virtual rollout, the team found itself on the wrong side of clunky Zoom meetings and frequent miscommunication.

Just twenty-four hours before the launch, Lina finally tracked down a colleague who had been evading her for days. He had totally dropped the ball on a few key deliverables they needed, and she worked non-stop to save the day. It was down to the wire, but Lina was able to bring the campaign flawlessly across the finish line.

How did I know it was flawless? This was a really well-known organization. So, unlike other projects my coaching clients work on, I had the unique privilege of watching this launch as a member of the general public. We stayed in close touch while Lina scrambled to tie everything up in a bow and then exchanged excited messages on Launch Day. That's why I was so confused when Lina called me for our coaching session a few days later in tears.

"Why don't you tell me what happened?" I asked her, as she took a few moments to grab a tissue and take a few deep breaths.

"Well," she explained, "I got onto the Zoom for our debrief this morning, and I told my boss how we had a little hiccup, but I got it resolved, and she had no appreciation for how hard I worked to make that happen. Can you believe that? This was supposed to be my moment to show everyone what I could do. Not only did I do it, but I saved us from a complete disaster in the process."

This launch meant so much to her, and she began crying again. It's my job as a coach to challenge, champion, support, and hold my clients accountable—and this was one of those moments where I had to say something to a client that can be hard to hear.

"A hiccup?" I asked her incredulously. "This wasn't a *hiccup*. A hiccup is when the Zoom link needs to be resent. This was a *crisis*. You identified it, you solved it, and the real win was that nobody felt a thing. But that's the problem, Lina. Nobody knows that because you told them that this was a *hiccup*, not a crisis that you resolved with incredible leadership and project management skills."

"Your boss responded to you like this was a nothing-burger because *you* made her believe it was a nothing-burger. She thinks there was a hiccup, and that's the response she gave you because she expects you to be able to handle the hiccups. So, you tell me: was this really a hiccup? Or was it a crisis?"

Lina needed to claim her voice, own her message, and educate her stakeholders—and she'd missed that opportunity. Luckily for her, she had a great working relationship with her boss and was able to go back and correct the record. Many of us, however, don't get that chance when we don't successfully own our message the first time around. Too many of us are out there, just like Lina was, with a bad case of the hiccups, and it's holding us back.

That's why, since that day Lina called me, I've coined "The Hiccup Test" when it comes to owning our message. Here's how it works:

- Are you clearly articulating your message, taking credit for your wins, and educating your stakeholders? Great, you've passed!
- Are you toning down your message for the sake of being humble, fear of rocking the boat or troubling anybody, or hoping your work will speak for itself? Calling, for example, something that was a full-fledged crisis a hiccup? Bad news, you've failed.

No sweat if you can look back on a time when you've failed The Hiccup Test—I can too, and it's exactly why we're here in this chapter.

UNDERSTANDING WHY IT'S (SO) HARD TO OWN OUR MESSAGE:

For many women, owning our message doesn't come easily. If this is you, rest assured: you are not alone. Below are three reasons that talented women often find it difficult to claim—and turn up the volume on—their voice at work.

#1. **Structural bias.** The Old Playbook simultaneously taught us to "not rock the boat *too* much" and artificially cheerleaded us with lazy "girl power" or "girl boss" messages like "just say your piece; it's not that hard." So let me be clear about something: I cannot underscore enough that struggling to claim your voice or own your message at work is *not your fault.* Decades of academic research, from institutions like Yale University, The University of Texas, and George Washington University have demonstrated that when we speak up, we're often subjected to backlash and diminishment at worst, and interruption or good old-fashioned mansplaining at best. Notably, because of the very nature of structural bias, women of color in particular often feel even more pressure around censoring, editing, or perfecting their messages.

#2. Old habits die hard. As we discussed at length in our *Ditching Perfectionism* chapter, so many of us have been socialized with "Good Girl" messages like, "Don't take up space," "Be humble," or "Don't speak out of turn." They're messages our Inner Critic has clung tightly to that have created deep-seated habits based on the fear that using our voices will hurt us. Of course, the structural bias we experience only compounds this. We cannot get ahead, however, *unless* we use our voice. When we stay quiet for fear of being punished by others, we are just punishing ourselves.

#3. The "Qualified Quiet." One of the biggest issues we have around owning our message at work is that too many of us believe our work should speak for itself. "Well, it does not," insists Meredith Fineman, author of *Brag Better: Master the Fearless Art of Self-Promotion.* As Fineman explains, many women fall into a group that she calls "the Qualified Quiet: a group of highly competent individuals who are under-estimated because they lack a strategy for self-promotion, thinking their work will speak for itself."

Owning Your Message: Writing Better Emails

With an estimated 300 billion emails sent a day, email is our *highest-volume* form of communication. Here are three tips to also make it your *highest-value* form of communication.

#1. BLOT. The average reader only spends 11 seconds per email—so don't waste them. Instead of starting your email with, "I hope this email finds you well," start with your BLOT: Bottom Line On Top. E.g., "I'm reaching out regarding next steps from our meeting."

#2. Rethink pleasantries. Moving pleasantries from the beginning of the email to the end often reads as more sincere. While starting an email with, "I hope you're doing well" can feel boilerplate, coupling pleasantries with a thank you at the end can often feel warmer. E.g., "Thanks again for your hard work on this/for help with this/for considering my request, and I hope you are doing well."

#3. Use a question to create a call to action. Do you want somebody to read your email or read *and* reply? If you're looking for a reply, it's critical to ensure you have a call to action. Consider the difference between simply stating, "If you could provide an update that would be great," vs. asking with a call to action, "Will you please provide an update?" Using a question isn't rude; it's getting the job done with effective communication.

Many women in the Qualified Quiet fear that self-promotion will be perceived as abrasive or flashy, leading them to underplay their hand at work: "If you have done the work, but you don't know how to talk about it and tout it—you're part of the Qualified Quiet. The Qualified Quiet occupy the other end of the spectrum from those who brag loudly without focus or adherence to truth. They have experience, but they don't know how to talk about it. They want more than they are currently getting, but they're afraid to say so."

FINDING YOUR VOICE AND FINDING YOUR GOALS

Priyanka came to me completely distraught. She was an expert in her field of food and nutrition policy but felt like she was watching everyone around her—with a fraction of her credentials and experience—get ahead of her at work. What really set her over the edge, however, was a group of consultants from a well-known global firm she called "the crew."

While Priyanka was cutting her teeth for years in her field in grad school and on Capitol Hill, "the crew" were career consultants who had been hopping from industry *du jour* to industry *du jour*. Now, they had pivoted to food and nutrition issues, and they were blowing up her LinkedIn feed.

She was jealous, and she wasn't ashamed to admit it.

She also felt frustrated: "Why are they able to create a bolder profile with a fraction of my experience? I've been looking for a new job for over a year and haven't found anything. Meanwhile, they're on panels, writing white papers, and in the rooms that I should be in."

The issue wasn't Priyanka's credentials or résumé, but the way she was *positioning* them.

First, she hadn't updated her LinkedIn profile for years. So we worked together to rewrite her LinkedIn "About Me" section. "Wow," I told her after she showed me the final copy, "you're so impressive." I'm very careful to not get clients hooked on *my* external validation, but these five new sentences—all of which simply reflected her credentials, impact, and passion—blew me away. With the new confidence in her profile, she felt emboldened to repost industry articles that she was reading and even write her own.

Okay, beginning to claim her voice on the internet? Check. Next came the live conversations that Priyanka, as an introvert, dreaded.

She was great when she was in a room with people she knew, but she felt uncomfortable talking about herself in networking situations—something that was holding her back in her job search.

Priyanka started preparing a list of questions when she went to networking breakfasts like, "What brought you here today?" instead of the more transactional, "What do you do?" as well as practicing (in advance) a few talking points she could fall back on, like discussing projects she was leading at work.

Slowly, between the baby steps on LinkedIn and in-person networking events, Priyanka was getting more comfortable owning her message, building her networking, refreshing dormant relationships, and getting more traction in her job search in the process.

But when she got to interviews, she was still using language like "we" and "helped" to describe projects she personally spearheaded. Like Lina's Hiccup Test, in an attempt to be humble, she was diminishing her contributions. This was classic "Qualified Quiet" material.

After a few interviews that didn't land her an offer, a network contact she had reconnected with since she began putting herself out there reached out with what looked like the "perfect job." They agreed on title, compensation, and a start date. All she needed was the final paperwork.

The finish line was in sight in early March 2020 when the pandemic hit, and the organization issued a sudden hiring freeze. Priyanka was beside herself and called me crying that evening after she got the call. "I'm so sorry this happened," I told her. "Sleep on it, and we'll work out a plan together tomorrow."

Priyanka sent out an email a few days later, letting the hiring manager know that she appreciated the bind the organization was in and reiterating her excitement about the opportunity as a perfect mutual fit. She ended the email by asking if they could speak again.

In her boldest move yet, when she got on the phone, Priyanka pitched an idea: "I know the budget is technically on the freeze, but *not* filling this role actually does more harm than good." She walked through a business case for why hiring her was actually both prudent and time-sensitive. "I'm happy to work with you on a flexible or extended start date if the organization needs more runway due to budget constraints. I just know this is a great mutual fit, and I want to work together."

The hiring manager wanted to hire Priyanka as much as Priyanka wanted the job. Moreover, she was blown away by Priyanka's initiative. Four weeks later, Priyanka had a start date.

Truly a dream job, it's where she's been ever since. Active as ever on social media where her work, her speaking engagements, and her ideas pass through my newsfeed weekly, I asked her a while ago what was happening with that pesky "crew" that once vexed her. "Oh," she replied, "you know, I haven't even thought about them in a while." She was too busy owning her message to be jealous of the way anybody else was owning theirs.

Owning Your Message: Cool It on the Exclamation Points

I often see women use exclamation points to demonstrate how friendly and warm they are (*"Please like me!!!!"*), given email's inherently cold and clinical format.

Larry Kim nailed it in *Inc.*: "Overusing this one piece of punctuation gives your communications a distinctly middle school flavor and kills your credibility." In addition to making you look over-eager or childish, "It makes you seem melodramatic and will give employers pause about allowing you to represent the company to partners or clients."

Exclamation point rule of thumb: You get one exclamation point per email, tops. Use it wisely.

CLAIMING YOUR VOICE AT WORK: FOR OURSELVES AND OTHERS

"Would you want your children to eat off a bathroom stall?" Christine Michel Carter asked her boss one day in a moment of extreme frustration and exhaustion. At twenty-five, she had just returned to work after the birth of her daughter, Maya.

The only Black woman at a startup staffed almost exclusively by white men, Carter worked on the marketing team. Her days consisted of attending marketing meetings, working on the company's marketing strategy, and pumping four times a day in a community stall in a shared, co-ed bathroom. Locking the door, strapping on her hands-free pumping bra, and balancing her Medela breast pump precariously on the seat so none of her pump parts would touch the floor or toilet, Carter sat on that restroom floor for hours daily.

Not only did Carter lack basic privacy and hygiene while providing sustenance for her daughter, she was also subjected to a front-row seat when anybody else came in to take care of their own private business. Pooping and pumping just were not a winning combination. In fact, it was completely disgusting. One day, as she was sitting on the bathroom floor, she looked around and said to herself, "This cannot be my life. This cannot be the solution."

Nobody seemed to think anything was wrong with this other than Carter. So she picked up the phone and called her boss, who worked in a different office, politely but firmly asking, "Would you want your child to be eating out of this area? Because this is where my child has to eat out of, and I have to take this home every day."

In the three weeks it took the company to accommodate Carter with a private and hygienic place to pump—which, it turned out, was *her legal right* from the start—her milk dried up. She was absolutely devastated. There was nothing she could do for herself, but she was resolute in her convictions: "I cannot let other women get to this point where you're fighting and fighting [for your legal right to pump in a private, hygienic, and safe location] for so long that your milk goes dry. It's pointless at that point for you to get the rights that you should have. I want you to know about them in advance so this doesn't happen to you."

Carter felt like she had learned about her rights too late, and her company had done nothing to make up for lost time: "Most marketers are writers at night… so, like many of my colleagues, at night, I started going back to what I love doing, which was writing." Carter started researching the rights of working parents and writing about her own experiences.

She was frustrated by all the bad career advice she was hearing—classic Old Playbook messages about her role inside the family and what was/wasn't feasible at work, "which was just so outdated and antiquated from older generations who didn't have to balance what I was trying to balance" as a career-focused mother.

As she got involved with Mom Congress—an advocacy organization focused on the public policy issues that impact moms—Carter was moved: "I was learning and hearing some of these heartbreaking stories around maternal mental health and learning other women's stories about caregiving as Black women or women of color."

It wasn't just about balancing babies and career. It was also the strain of caring for aging parents that touched her in addition to the other lived experiences she was hearing about. Each catalyzed her to continue writing and speaking: "It was just frustration after frustration, and I started voicing those frustrations on social media and being no holds barred with some of the articles I was writing."

While so many women self-censor to make their messages more pleasing, Carter was passionate about capturing the authentic (and, at times, raw) experiences of the other working moms she was hearing from. That's when Carter caught the attention of then-Senator Kamala Harris who wanted to meet Carter to discuss her position on the Maternal Care Act.

Working at her day job, caring for two small children, dialing up her role as an advocate, and serving as a policy advisor to US Senators didn't leave Carter much free time. But she loved writing and had an idea for a different kind of "mom-lit" novel. After working on the manuscript for over a year with an agent and a contract from a publishing house in the bag, Carter walked away from her book deal.

Her voice was her power, and she was concerned about it being sanitized inside a traditional publishing house. Unfortunately, that wasn't a surprise to her: "I run into that self-censoring from mothers, especially Black mothers, so often. My book, *MOM AF*, is the first mom-lit book written by a Black mom, and I had to self-publish because people wanted to censor my words. They even wanted to censor the title."

But Carter trusted her ideas and her voice: "I'm really glad that I went ahead and published it myself… because the book resonates so much more with mothers. I wanted to tell—and at the heart of what I always do is to always tell—the honest story of motherhood." Her book went on to be a top seller.

There was no doubt Carter found her voice. A decade after she first fought for a clean place to pump and cried over her milk drying up, she has become one of the world's most recognized thought leaders on working motherhood, a best-selling author, a *Forbes* contributor, an entrepreneur, and a global advocate for women.

So what's her secret? For Carter, owning her message has been part science (relying on everything she knew about marketing) and part art (relying on the "God-given intuition" she believes we all possess). She reminds us that owning our message is not a set-it-and-forget-it thing like programming your thermostat. It is an ongoing act of claiming your voice and using it.

She reminds us that when we find our voices, we don't only advance our own goals, dreams, and passions. We often find opportunities to help other women in our orbit move forward with *their* goals, dreams, and passions.

Owning Your Message: Sorry, Not Sorry

Take a moment and consider how many times you've started an email with "sorry for the delay" or "sorry to bug you." What were you trying to achieve?

Omitting "sorry" doesn't make our emails rude. It prevents us from undermining ourselves and keeps our emails confident and direct. Here are three tips for owning your message with a sorry-not-sorry mindset:

#1. Say thank you. Instead of "sorry for the delay," try "thanks for waiting" or "thanks for your patience."

#2. Say nothing. Most of the time, we apologize for things that don't require an apology. Instead of starting with any kind of apology or "sorry substitute," simply begin your idea, email, or meeting.

#3. Save sorry for when you mean it. Apologies become hollow when they're handed out like candy on Halloween. When you do something that requires an apology, make it direct, concise, and personal. Once you have taken accountability and proposed a remedy, you can move forward.

THE NEW PLAYBOOK FOR OWNING YOUR MESSAGE

As our bragging guru Meredith Fineman reminds, "You are amazing, and I want everyone to know it... If you're not enthusiastic about your achievements, nobody else can be." It's a battle cry for us all to own our voice at work and turn up the volume—sharing our ideas, amplifying our impact, advancing our careers, and augmenting our influence. Below are five tools for writing the New Playbook on owning your message at work.

> **#1. Trust Your Intuition.** Carter sees intuition as absolutely foundational to owning her message: "There's something to be said for the God-given intuition that we all have. I trust it, and it leads me. If you want to own your message, you cannot ignore your intuition."

Often, as Carter explains, we *already know* intuitively what we want to say:

> *It's that thing that's keeping you up at night and gnawing at you about whatever experience you're having at work—and you're silencing yourself because you think that's the 'right thing to do.' Or it's the fact that you have this creative passion inside of you, and you're not following it because 'it's not the right time.' That's what you're telling yourself, but your intuition is telling you something different. It will continue to gnaw at you until you listen to it.*

When we tap into our intuition, we tap into our fullest ability to both own our message and live authentically as a result: "The relief that you feel once you own your message?

The weight of the world is off of your shoulders. If for no other reason, you have to own your message, you have to use your voice to pursue your passions, or else it will keep you up at night. We're able to tap into our voice when we allow ourselves to tap into our intuition."

#2. The "I Forbid It" List. The simplicity of tapping into our intuition is that the words often find *us* if we tune in. Unfortunately, as we covered in our *Reclaiming Our Intuition* chapter, too many of us have been trained to tune out. As a result, too often, we rely on "hedging" and "crutch" language to soften our delivery, reduce the risk of a "bad idea," or to be "polite." These bad habits don't move us forward; they undermine us. That's why, in order to own your message, I have created this list of sixteen words and phrases I forbid you to say at work (you can also download a printable copy to keep at your desk at www.somethingmajorcoaching.com/book).

Forbidden when sharing your ideas:
1. You've probably already thought of this…
2. Maybe I'm missing something…
3. This might be a dumb idea…
4. You all know more about this than I do…
5. Have we thought about…? (Pro tip: Phrasing your awesome idea as a question is basically inviting somebody else to take credit for it)
6. I'm no expert, but…
7. Using "we" instead of "I"
8. You all have been working on this longer than I have…

Forbidden crutch words:
   9. Just
  10. Actually
  11. Maybe
  12. I wanted to…
  13. Sorry

Forbidden when receiving praise:
  14. It was nothing
  15. Just happy to help

Forbidden when not emailing back instantaneously:
  16. Sorry for the delay

Using hedging and crutch language is like intentionally hitting a single when our ideas and contributions could be a grand slam—or *at least* a double. Here are a few suggestions to help break bad habits and choose your words wisely:

- **Just blurt.** Seriously, I want you to practice just blurting out your ideas. That means in a meeting, you can drop your disclaimers and just share your perspective. In an email, you can get to the point with "I'm writing to follow-up on…" versus "I just wanted to check in to see how things were going with…" You can also share your ideas in a statement instead of couching them in a question.

- **Hit the delete button.** Pay attention to this especially around your hedge words like "just," "actually," or whatever softening crutch word is your personal kryptonite. In emails, don't send your note until you review it and *actually hit that delete button* on those hedges and crutches. In meetings, practice speaking up intentionally with a focus on (mentally) deleting these words from your talk track. You can even try jotting down your talking points in advance if it helps, or find a trusted ally in the room who can listen to you speak up and share feedback on how you sounded.

- **Say thank you.** Had a great idea and got some recognition? Hallelujah! Now just say thank you. Don't tell them it was nothing. Don't use "we" instead of "I." Simply say these two words: thank you.

- **Save sorry.** Remember, every time you issue an unnecessary apology, you are cutting yourself down. Instead, you can say, "thanks for your patience," or simply say nothing at all.

#3. Channel Your Inner "Challenger." Growing up professionally in sales, I read the Bible and preached its gospel regularly to my direct reports and the teams I trained. I'm not talking about *that* Bible, but the other one: *The Challenger Sale*. Here are the cliffs notes:

- Studying over 100,000 B2B sales professionals, Matthew Dixon, alongside co-author Brent Adamson and their research team at the Corporate Executive Board, identified five types of salespeople, notably including "Relationship-Builders" and "Challengers."
- As the authors explain, it turned out that, "Relationship Builders were reactive, responsive, generous, and all

that good stuff generous is, but they actually finished dead last when you look at high performers."

- It was Challengers who blew their peers out of the water, using a three-pronged approach: teach, tailor, take control.

Since I left sales, I've been teaching my clients for years to channel their inner Challenger and teach-tailor-and-take-control their way to owning their message. After all, you may not be selling a product or service, but you are selling your ideas. Here's how it works:

- **Teach:** The first thing Challengers do, Dixon explained during our interview, is teach the customer something new, "almost grabbing them by their lapels and kind of shaking them out of their comfort zone." Think of the way that Priyanka started *teaching* people about her accomplishments and how she *taught* the hiring manager why she needed to hire Priyanka, even though she was on a budget freeze. The best teaching creates what Dixon called a "constructive tension"—illuminating a blind spot that your stakeholders haven't seen before that they now can't ignore—and positioning *your* ideas as the remedy to that. When Priyanka told the hiring manager what the costs were going to be to the organization, that was a moment of constructive tension she relieved by making her hiring the solution.

- **Tailor:** "The second thing the Challenger does," Dixon explained, "is they tailor their message." In the kinds of consensus-driven sales Dixon studied, it really came down to a game of "herding cats." Challengers excelled at tailoring their message to every member of the group who'd be involved in a consensus decision. So consider this: if you've ever positioned yourself for a raise, promotion, or requesting additional headcount, *you've* been part of a "consensus sale." If you've ever interviewed for a new job, *you've* been part of a consensus sale. Tailoring your message to all the stakeholders involved in any decision is key to owning your message.

- **Take control:** Finally, Challengers were not afraid to take control and drive the next steps. As Dixon clarified, "It doesn't mean they're rude, aggressive, or obnoxious. But make no mistake, they do hold their ground when somebody pushes back. They don't immediately cave in the face of skepticism or wilt in the face of pushback. Challengers see cognitive dissonance not as an imperative to retreat, but as an opportunity for intellectual exploration." Think back to Lina and her boss, Priyanka and her hiring manager, Carter and… well, the whole world. Each one of them took control in sustaining and redirecting the conversation as needed. They took control, certainly, but they also taught their stakeholders and tailored their conversations along the way.

- **But isn't relationship-building… good?** When interviewed for this book, Dixon reiterated something that I often explain to my clients who feel uncomfortable channeling their Inner Challenger and ask, "Wait, shouldn't I be a Relationship-Builder?" As Dixon makes clear, "When we say that Relationship-Builders finished dead last, it doesn't mean relationships don't matter. It means that the *currency* of the relationship has actually changed. It's not enough today to be likable, generous, responsive, and reactive"—something we've all learned by living our lives through the rules of the Old Playbook. Challengers, Dixon confirms, forge the strongest, stickiest, and most influential relationships by using their insights (not just likeability) to influence decision-making.

This is why, for years, I've been preaching the gospel: telling my clients to teach-tailor-and-take-control their way to influence. Whether you are negotiating salary, sharing an idea at work, or even interviewing for a job, aren't you just selling an idea? Channeling your inner Challenger is one of the best ways to own your message.

#4. When in Doubt, Just Look at the Facts. One thing I consistently observe in brilliant women is our tendency to overcomplicate things. Again, please file under "Not Your Fault," as we have addressed a lot of the perfectionistic and Inner Critic programming that drives this. This was the case for Blake, a senior marketing executive at a Fortune 500 company who was constantly second-guessing how she should speak up at work, at board meetings, and on social media. She was mired in self-doubt spirals of "am I worthy?" and "am I bragging?"

At our coaching sessions, we decided to temporarily side-step the "feels"—not because they weren't important, but because they weren't helpful—and just look at facts. Yes, she was worthy. Otherwise, she wouldn't have that board seat to begin with or that track record in her field. No, she wasn't bragging; making sure her team's accomplishments are recognized in the company is a core responsibility for advancing her people, securing more budget, and supporting her team's mission. Similarly, being visible on social media was as mainstream as "branding" and "relationship-building" gets these days. Within three months of simply looking at (and speaking about) the facts, Blake elevated key members of her team, rescoped her department's mission, and demonstrated its value despite budget cuts. Outside of work, she also became more vocal in board meetings.

When you're feeling insecure or tongue-tied about owning your message, I encourage you to simply look at the facts, asking yourself questions like:

- What do I *do* at work day-to-day?
- What parts of my job am I best at or most excited about?
- Where/how do others feel the impact of my work?
- What do I have experience or expertise in?
- Pro tip: the answers to your next social media post, your next professional bio, or your next opportunity to claim credit for a job well-done all live inside those questions.

#5. Embrace Owning Your Message as a Team Sport.
Great news: you do not have to own your message all on your own. Just as important as claiming your voice is building a squad of advocates and allies who can help you amplify it.

There is a famous story in Washington, DC, about the early days of the Obama administration. A cadre of female aides felt like they were being constantly spoken over by male colleagues in meetings with the president, so they banded together and created a strategy called "amplification." As *The Washington Post* reported:

> *When a woman made a key point, other women would repeat it, giving credit to its author. This forced the men in the room to recognize the contribution—and denied them the chance to claim the idea as their own. 'We just started doing it, and made a purpose of doing it. It was an everyday thing,' said one former Obama aide who requested anonymity to speak frankly. Obama noticed, she and others said, and began calling more often on women and junior aides.*

Amplification is just one example of how you can make owning your message a team sport. While speaking out, speaking up, and claiming space for your ideas and contributions is key, so is enfranchising others around you—whether that's asking somebody to share or comment on your LinkedIn post, to put in a good word with a stakeholder they know, or asking a client to send a note to *your boss* when you've done something awesome. I've done this countless times, and trust me, it works wonders. In fact, one client even tried to hire me away from my own boss!

Owning our message can be hard, but it's also tremendously empowering and utterly career-changing. The next time you speak up, ask yourself, "Does this pass The Hiccup Test, or am I over-editing myself with self-censoring language? What do I have to contribute that the world needs to hear? What do I need to say to get what I rightfully deserve?"

In a world where we're obsessed with our work (more on that in our next chapter), we're seriously lacking when it comes to the vocabulary to describe the *impact* of that work. Owning your message doesn't make you abrasive. It makes you powerful. Your words matter, so use them wisely.

CHAPTER 8:

REASSESSING PRODUCTIVITY AND RECLAIMING TIME

———

"The truth is I girl-bossed too close to the sun, and I got burnt," Liz told me one night over tacos and tequila on a perfect summer night in Los Angeles.

Fresh off a layoff and a year out from a divorce, Liz felt like she could "finally breathe and enjoy [her] life" in a way she hadn't ever given herself permission to do before.

By thirty-five, she had "worked her ass off," notching more career accomplishments than most people do in a lifetime. She got her dream job during the hand-over-fist-growth years for one of the world's major ride-hailing apps: "I was a Manager for one of the country's largest regions, with an annual budget of over $30 million. It was exciting, and I thought that excitement was why I was working all the time."

To this day, Liz will tell you that the job was "the most fun I've ever had." But as the company matured and Liz moved on, she took her hustle-and-grind 24/7 habits with her to a prestigious think tank before rolling the dice on another startup across the country.

She worked constantly: "The truth is, I thought my career was my identity, but my career was my *employer's identity*. It was also a place where I hid out from a relationship that I knew was never right." Grinding it out constantly, Liz was always producing: answering every last email, squeezing in that extra meeting when her calendar was already stacked, and working the extra hour to pound out one more item on her to-do list.

Fifteen years into her career, this was the only way Liz knew how to work. She believed if she *did* it all, she would *have* it all. But, as too many women learn the hard way, that is an unsustainable fallacy.

In a stroke of luck (if you can ever call a layoff "lucky"), just as she was making plans to give her notice and quit the start-up, she got the news that they were letting *her* go, severance package and all. "This was the fresh start I needed, and now I'm getting paid for it," she told me as she took another sip of her spicy margarita.

Liz had been trapped inside the myth that if we can do it all, we'll achieve our dreams. If we're not careful, however, we end up living inside a nightmare.

I've watched too many women wake up from this nightmare (most without the same golden parachute Liz had) only to find themselves in crisis. That's exactly why reassessing our productivity and reclaiming our time is so urgent in a work world that never slows down.

THE PRODUCTIVITY LIE

Let's get real about something important: obsessing over our "productivity" isn't pushing us forward. It's holding us back, and it's running us absolutely ragged in the process.

Too many of us *are* working hard—often white-knuckling through each day, project, or quarter, just like Liz was. So why aren't we getting ahead?

The answer is something Mother Honestly (MH) Founder and CEO Blessing Adesiyan calls "The Productivity Lie."

This is the notion that "in order to be productive and do good work, we need to have butts in seats, constantly getting work done." Our culture, Adesiyan notes, measures productivity through the lens of the privileged white male experience: a lived experience that is unencumbered by the same standards (and time commitments) that women face from both office work and domestic housework.

The Productivity Lie, Adesiyan argues, does not leave room for a vision of productivity as defined through the spectrum of women's lived experiences, let alone "through the spectrum of single mothers, women of color, and LGBTQ+ women… It's measuring productivity based on an unattainable ideal that somebody is able to unplug from distractions to hone his skills and get ahead. Meanwhile, women are being crushed by the demands of the home. It affects our goals and dreams."

That's exactly how the Productivity Lie traps us in a cycle of constantly striving and struggling to prove ourselves: feeling like we're always playing catch up and often exhausting ourselves in the process.

It's a tension that Adesiyan herself has lived and learned first-hand through her career as a chemical engineer turned entrepreneur and mother of four in our always-on culture.

"I distinctly remember setting the alarm clock to 4:00 a.m. every morning," Adesiyan said while reflecting on her first job as a chemical engineer. "I would wake up at 4:00 a.m. just to get myself and my daughter ready so that we were out of the house by 5:30 a.m. ... In fact, I'd often be waiting outside the daycare by 5:45 a.m. so that I could drop her off as soon as they opened the doors at 6:00 a.m. This way I could be at my desk at work by 6:30 a.m."

A divorced, single mom—and the only woman of color on her team—she went to work daily surrounded by a team of mostly white men. There was no doubt in Adesiyan's mind that "we've structured our society in a way that was not built for us. Not for women, not for people of color, not for single moms, not for the LGBTQ+ [community]."

As the daycare drop-offs and years went by, on paper, Adesiyan was thriving. With a CV that boasted seemingly every dominant player in her field, she was steadily climbing the corporate ladder. Along the way, she also remarried and went on to have three more children.

But like so many women, in her quest to "have it all," Adesiyan was always living on the razor's edge that the Productivity Lie creates: getting it all done, but by the skin of her teeth. She was so burdened by the productivity standards in her personal, professional, and family life that there was no margin for error.

The Productivity Lie required flawless choreography. But on February 20, 2020—unbeknownst to her, the last day she would ever work in a corporate office—Adesiyan missed a step in the perfect dance that was required to simply get through each day.

After another grueling day at work, she began her commute home: a bus ride to a parking lot, where she'd pick up her car and drive herself home, where four children were waiting for her to start the homework-dinner-bath time-bedtime routine.

On the way though, she spilled the breast milk that she'd pumped at the office—the *liquid gold* that required her to claw for a few free pumping breaks each day on her uber-productive, back-to-back schedule.

She unraveled, sobbing into her iPhone camera with her blinker on and mascara rolling down her cheeks. Her confessional would later go viral. "I'm just tired," she cried, still managing to make her turn as the light turned green, "I pumped eighteen ounces of milk today, and it's all gone. I'm hooked up right now [to a portable breast pump] trying to pump on my way home. I couldn't even pump on the bus because there was no freaking outlet. All of this is just too much right now. There *has* to be a better way."

Weeks later, as COVID-19 swept the nation, like Americans everywhere, Adesiyan was locked down inside her home with her family. Initially, it looked like her life could be more "flexible." At least, that's what it seemed like on paper.

To start, she relished the fact that she could nurse her son daily instead of pumping, bottle-feeding, and doing the staggering amount of cleaning required to keep pump parts and bottles sanitary in the process.

Soon, however, it became clear that working from home brought its own crushing version of the Productivity Lie with it. "Because we were working remotely," Adesiyan explains, "there was a sense of 'You should be grateful, and you should always be on and available.'" It became clear to Adesiyan that there was "no room for error. We now needed to deliver even more."

This left her feeling like she had to constantly prove that she was working (something called "Performative

Productivity Culture," which we'll explore later in this chapter). While it was exhausting, like successful women everywhere, Adesiyan is extraordinarily resilient and, initially, made her peace with it: "I was working around the clock, and I was okay with that because I knew I could at least take a break and make lunch for the kids."

As quickly as she realized these moments were the one thing that *was* working for her in all of this, she realized it was *not* working for her boss.

Adesiyan went out of her way to clarify when she *wasn't* available daily (when she was caring for her children at breakfast, lunch, dinner, and bedtime) and when she *was* available—which was basically all other times.

One night, despite being clear that she was stepping away from her computer to cook dinner for her family, her boss began relentlessly texting her about a totally non-urgent issue. He made his expectation clear that she would be available, and he was clearly annoyed—both that she was not online to manage the issue *and* that she was holding firm on a boundary.

As Adesiyan recalls, "I addressed the situation, but I felt violated." It became her breaking point as she realized, "I cannot work in an environment where I don't feel valued, and nobody trusts me. When you've worked your way to a senior leadership position at a Fortune 100 company, and then you're being asked to 'prove yourself' every single second of the day? That was not sitting right with me."

Despite an extraordinary track record and a love for chemical engineering, Adesiyan started the process of tendering her resignation. "What was most unfortunate is that I was not the only one," she reflects, referring to the millions of other women who left the workforce during the pandemic.

Many of these women have either returned to the workforce at a slower pace than other demographics or never returned at all, according to the National Women's Law Center.

Already running her business MH part-time—a platform designed to make the world more equitable for working caregivers and to propel women forward in motherhood, work, and life—Adesiyan decided to take her business full-time. The business thrived, and in less than two years after she'd quit, MH was reaching over one million parents.

Not only has she achieved incredible success as the number of both caregivers and employers who count on MH's platform has grown hand over fist, but her perspective has shifted as she has chucked out the Old Playbook in favor of a new one: "The old rules are about cranking work out—constantly producing—and those things are ridiculous. My [new] view of productivity is prioritizing my wellbeing, producing high-quality work when I'm getting work done, and centering care. I've created an environment where I can truly thrive... embedded in my mission and my work, not constantly looking over my shoulders told to always be available."

UNDERSTANDING PERFORMATIVE PRODUCTIVITY CULTURE

You don't have to be a mom or a chemical engineer to relate to Adesiyan's story. That's because we live in a culture that valorizes overwork and busywork as a status symbol—not just doing the work itself, but *appearing* to do the work—and it's toxic.

It's also what I call Performative Productivity Culture: a system of workplace habits where *performing* our commitment to hustle-and-grind culture takes precedence over the *impact* of our contributions.

It often looks like attending superfluous meetings or answering every email, Slack message, or IM that comes our way immediately. It can also look like being afraid to have a yellow or red light next to your name and keeping yourself marked as constantly available. It looks like responding to an email that can go out in the morning just because you received it at 9:00 p.m. (or maybe because you want to *show* that you're checking your emails at 9:00 p.m.).

Too often, I've heard women come to coaching and tell me that they just "need to be more productive." But something doesn't compute here because the women who are telling me this aren't (a) *habitual procrastinators* who are constantly missing deadlines, (b) *habitual deadline-missers* who are constantly being fired from jobs for their underperformance, or (c) *habitual slackers* who are getting by on the bare minimum. Here are three ways our Performative Productivity Culture holds us back:

#1. It's distracting us from doing meaningful work. One report published by *CNBC* demonstrated that skilled office workers are spending only a third of their time doing the actual work they were hired to do. A mere third—that's *horrifying*. So what are we doing with the rest of our time? According to the reported study, which was conducted by the project management and workflow platform Asana, nearly all of that remaining time is spent doing the "work around work." That includes sitting in pointless meetings that were held because we were too busy to do the planning required to make them productive, answering messages immediately, and constantly losing time as we switch between tasks (something that is actively decreasing our attention spans, *CNBC* reports).

#2. It's stifling our innovation and creativity. One of the biggest costs of our Performative Productivity Culture is that we've mistaken constant availability for meaningful work, and it's crushing creativity and innovation. In fact, we're so busy performing productivity—literally singing for our supper—that we deprive ourselves of the unstructured, uninterrupted time known as "deep work" that is required to do our best work.

#3. It denies us rest. In our Performative Productivity Culture, there is never time to unplug. Dr. Melissa Mazmanian, a professor of informatics at the University of California Irvine, reminds us that when Blackberries were first introduced two decades ago, "it registered as a superpower." Today, however, "the superpower [has] morphed into an obligation," creating "a spiral of expectations" in the process. That's why over a third of Americans don't feel like they have a concrete end to their day, and a whopping 40 percent of Americans also believe that burnout is "inevitable."

We must find ways to unhook from our engrained productivity beliefs, which can be especially hard when so many of us, it turns out, actually procrastinate inside our productivity.

Rethinking Meeting Culture on Your Team

Meetings are one of the biggest pain points inside our Performative Productivity Culture. As you look to shift the culture on your team, here are two questions you can ask before every meeting to ensure the team is doing good work—not doing busy work or busy trying to *perform* good work.

- **Is there an agenda for this meeting?** Meetings are important tools for collaboration… when they are done right. That's why teams that care about using meetings for doing good work versus performing it should send out an agenda twenty-four hours in advance, including meeting objectives, individual stakeholder responsibilities, and any pre-read materials. This is particularly effective for unlocking the best contributions from your introverts (whose best ideas you might currently be missing out on).
- **Which meetings can be replaced by a well-written email?** Amazon is infamous for banning Power-Point decks in favor of well-written memos. Too often, in our prove-I'm-busy culture, meetings are called for the sole purpose of informing: the pinnacle of performing the work instead of doing it. Informing can be done, and often done better, using the written word as opposed to a sixty-minute video call. Note: If visuals are an absolute must, consider adding a pre-recorded five-minute video with your note.

THREE REASONS WOMEN PROCRASTINATE
INSIDE PRODUCTIVITY

Is it possible that you're *procrastinating* inside your productivity? It's a question I've asked countless high-achieving women over the years—and one I now need you to consider.

While it feels insanely counterintuitive, it's also insanely common. That's because staying busy all the time is a great way to hide out from some of the things that scare us the most. Here are three reasons I often see high-performing women procrastinate inside their so-called productivity:

#1. We're hiding out from how overwhelmed we are.
It sounds crazy that we would make ourselves *more* overwhelmed when we're feeling overwhelmed in the first place, right? That was my reaction to research from Dr. Ashley Whillans, the author of *Time Smart* and a professor at Harvard Business School. According to Whillans, who studies the relationship between happiness and how we use our time, it's incredibly common:

> *When we feel time poor, we take on small, easy-to-complete tasks because they help us feel more control over our time. We think, there, made a protein shake and finished that errand. I'm getting stuff done! In this case, it's a false sense of control that doesn't alleviate the root cause of our busyness.*

Instead of finding ways to pare down our calendars, commitments, and to-do lists, we hide from the hard work of making the lifestyle changes that would *reduce* our to-do lists—focusing instead on the often meaningless things we can check off as "small wins." This is a false sense of control that keeps us procrastinating inside our so-called productivity.

#2. We're hiding out from our perfectionism. As we discussed previously, staying busy all the time in the pursuit of perfection doesn't keep us thriving— and we shouldn't mistake it for striving. It keeps us cocooned in a false sense of security because being "busy" feels safe. As Ladies Get Paid Founder Claire Wasserman noted in our *Ditching Perfectionism* chapter, overwork helps us "avoid the real work and the potential judgment that goes along with it." Being "busy" all the time is, too often, a convenient way to avoid confronting our perfectionism and the insecurity that lives inside of it.

#3. We're hiding out from finding out what *actually* makes us happy. The third reason why women procrastinate inside their productivity is, perhaps, the most tender reason of all. As Whillans notes, too often, "We keep ourselves overwhelmed in the hopes that this busyness will provide us fulfillment. Ironically, perpetual busyness undermines the goals that we set out to achieve with our busyness in the first place." As one former client, Julie, a partner at a Big Four Tax Firm remarked, "This one is *totally* me, but, if I'm being honest, I'd barely call this 'procrastination.' For years, it's been straight-up avoidance because asking these questions were just too scary."

To Send or Not to Send?

Emails can be a major driver of after-hours work (and stress), so below are two ideas to shift email culture on your team:

#1. Rethinking: "You don't need to answer right away!" Despite caveats like that one, research shows that senders of after-hours, non-urgent emails consistently *underestimate* how stressful those messages were for recipients, while recipients consistently *overestimate* how quickly they need to reply. If the matter is important but not urgent, use the delay send function (available on Outlook, Slack, and G-Suite) for working hours. If sending that message is to *prove* you're working, you're part of the problem. Remember, if something can be handled by firing off a message while you're watching Netflix, it's actually not urgent.

#2. Rethinking: Shared Quiet Hours. In the era of maximum flexibility, new research shows a critical finding on the power of shared quiet (or meeting-free, disruption-free) time: do-not-disturb policies on teams *only* work when they're shared or honored by all. Where could you design these with your team? Is there an email cut-off time? A shared no-meeting day or block weekly? Setting these expectations as a leader for your team—and honoring them—is critical to protecting this deep work time for your employees.

Because a to-do list is rarely completed—at least, for more than a single moment in time—we are consistently getting busier and busier, no matter how much we cross off. This vicious cycle provides a convenient (and sneaky) way to hide out inside our productivity, burrowing deeper inside the Old Playbook's Productivity Lie and Performative Productivity Culture in the process.

So how do we break the cycle? The key is to reprioritize being impactful instead of productive.

PRODUCTIVE VS. IMPACTFUL

"I just don't feel productive enough," Danielle told me at our first coaching session. "It's like I'm never getting enough done in the day."

Just a few months prior, things couldn't have been going better for her. Ever since her daughter had been born two years before, Danielle "desperately wanted to be closer to family." However, as a museum educator, most of the jobs that would be perfect for Danielle (on paper, at least) were located in distant, coastal cities—not in the Midwest, where Danielle grew up. So when she was offered the opportunity to serve as Executive Director at an art museum (the institution's chief leadership role) just twenty minutes away from her parents' home, she was ecstatic.

Shifting from a career in museum education to being the head of a museum was a huge shift for her—but it's also exactly what she had been preparing for over the course of her career.

What she hadn't prepared for, a mere seven weeks into her directorship, was the unprecedented choice to close the museum's doors due to COVID-19. Suddenly, the need to figure it all out and then *do it all* was crushing: "With a million things I *needed* to accomplish, being productive was at the top of my mind. I kept telling myself that I just needed to get the little things out of the way before I could focus on the big things."

Danielle was swirling as she was describing it all to me back then, so I asked her a simple question: "Is it more important that you be productive or impactful?"

"And that just hit me in the face in a good way," she explains now. "It made me completely stop because it *just made sense*." Danielle was, by her own admission, totally enmeshed in Procrastinating Inside Your Productivity Myth #1—she was hiding out from how overwhelmed she was:

> *I felt like there were so many big picture things that I needed to wrap my head around, from closing a multi-million-dollar capital campaign to reorganizing the staffing structure, to managing the museum during the pandemic. Those are big weighty topics that take time and thinking, and they weren't questions that had a single right answer.*

> *Being able to check off little things like, 'Did I figure out where the file was or create the new grant login?' felt like things I could manage. But then, at the end of the day, I'd look back at what I accomplished and ask myself, 'Did it move us forward?' Too often, that answer was no.*

This only made Danielle even more stressed out. But the Impactful, Not Productive mindset gave her a method of reframing.

Previously, taking time to think through questions like this felt like a luxury—nay, an extravagant indulgence: "There is so much pressure to do things quickly that it can seem like a privilege instead of an imperative to take our time. Especially when the world is constantly buzzing with email notifications. I learned that setting aside time isn't frivolous—it's critical." So she enlisted three tools to put the mindset shift into action.

- **First was a mantra.** "Just pausing to ask myself, *Does this decision make me productive or impactful?* helped me reevaluate my priorities and not automatically get caught in bad habits."

- **Second was blocking off serious think time.** "Every day, I try to block off one or two hours to make sure I have time to do the things that are important and that are going to be impactful, or so I can adjust my schedule without blowing it up." Danielle didn't know how important this was to her until people started scheduling over it. "I'd accept a meeting invitation because I felt guilty and then regret it," Danielle recalls. "I realized I needed to keep these blocks sacred, so I simply hit the decline button. I also started marking the blocks private, explaining to a few key people what they were, hoping to both be clear about the boundaries and also model this as a leader to them."

- **Lastly was accountability.** Just like sharing the "what" and "why" of her flex time blocks with a trusted circle of direct reports, she shared this goal with a few key people in her life, including her husband.

It didn't just move the dial for her but for the institution as a whole. With her head out of organizing the digital filing systems ("Impactful Danielle" hired a consultant) and managing the grant login tracking ("Impactful Danielle" delegated that to her development team), Danielle was able to do the community-oriented work she signed up to do. She went on to oversee a successful reopening of the museum, launch some of the most audacious and eventually award-winning exhibitions the museum had ever held, and steward a record-breaking corporate donation that would invest directly into community access to the museum.

Despite her success, Danielle is the first to note that the move from Productive to Impactful isn't a panacea; it's a practice: "There are times I fall off the wagon, but I've also learned that I know how to jump back on, and I now have the confidence—and the routines in place—to do that."

THE NEW PLAYBOOK FOR REASSESSING PRODUCTIVITY AND RECLAIMING TIME:

Rethinking "productivity" and reclaiming how we spend our time can have a tremendously positive impact on our lives. As Danielle notes, this goal takes practice and here are five tools to get you started:

#1. **Choose "Productive" or "Impactful."** The key isn't to expect that we'll ever stop having obligations but to manage them without falling into an inevitability mindset around "busyness." That's why it's critical to make a choice about whether we want to be a "productive worker" or an "impactful leader," just like Danielle did. Consider the difference between both mindsets:

The "Productive" Mindset	The "Impactful" Mindset
Must complete my to-do list	Must do the things that matter
Must do it all	Must do it well
Believes it's easier to "just do it myself"	Makes a plan to ensure successful execution as a team sport
Success is defined by completion	Success is defined by results

Before you default to tackling the next thing on your to-do list, I challenge you to check in with yourself: where could you bring an impactful mindset to work today instead of a productive one? What effect will that have on both your career and your happiness? Spoiler: it's impactful contributors who often get ahead, whereas productive contributors get saddled with more office housework.

#2. Ditch Time Confetti. A term coined by *New York Times* best-selling author, Brigid Schulte, Time Confetti is the phenomenon by which we *overestimate* how busy we are by *underestimating* how much of our time is lost to "bits of seconds and minutes [of] unproductive multitasking." Sure, most of us could definitely use more leisure time. But as researchers who study time like Harvard's Dr. Whillans point out, the bigger problem is that we're insidiously leaking the limited amounts of time we *do* have.

To see how it works, consider this scenario: after a long day of work, you have forty-five minutes all to yourself. Perhaps you sit down to read a book or watch an episode of your favorite show on Netflix.

A few minutes go by, and you hear the phone buzz, so you pick it up and see an email from work. It doesn't require a response, so you put it down. About five minutes later, it buzzes again, and this is an easy one to answer: yes, you *do* plan to be at the meeting tomorrow at 10:00 a.m., so you respond just to keep things moving with the team. While you're in there, you send back a "Yup, sounds great, thanks!" response to that other non-urgent email that came a few minutes before because you're already there, right?

About fifteen minutes later, your phone dings: a text from your best friend confirming if you're still on for Saturday night. "Yes, let's do it. Can't wait!" you reply back with a heart emoji. While the phone is in your hand, you do a quick check to see what has come in on Slack and Teams, and while you're doing that, your sister texts asking about the plans for Thanksgiving, so you text back super quickly that you'll call her tomorrow (again, with a heart emoji).

Another little while goes by, and an alarm goes off on your phone reminding you that tomorrow is your dad's birthday. You snooze the reminder for 8:00 a.m. tomorrow when you plan to call him, and while your phone is open, you pop over to Instagram and Twitter before you even realize your thumb has swiped up on the screen. After a minute or two of scrolling, you remember you want to get back to your book/show, so you put the phone down and finish out the last twenty minutes of your leisure block.

As Whillans explains, "Each bit alone seems not very bad. Collectively, though, all that confetti adds up to something more pernicious than you might expect." Check out how it all adds up:

Activity	Time Allotment
Email	120 seconds
Slack	15 seconds
Teams/Office IM	15 seconds
Texts	90 seconds
Alarm	5 seconds
Instagram	60 seconds
Twitter	60 seconds
Total amount of leisure time shredded by time confetti	*6 minutes, 5 seconds*

An email here and a text there don't seem like a lot. But in this scenario, they added up to six minutes and five seconds, which is nearly 15 percent of the entire forty-five minutes of leisure time you carved out for yourself.

Not only does Time Confetti diminish the *quantity* of our leisure time we have, but it also diminishes the *quality* of our leisure time. Instead of forty-five minutes all to ourselves to relax or unwind, we ricochet back and forth from chunks of mindless scrolling to turning on our work brains, to trying to get back to our leisure activity. In our efforts to relax, we insidiously only further exhaust ourselves.

#3. Carve Out Time for Fighting Fires. For many of the women I've coached throughout the years, the only thing that is predictable about their jobs is the *unpredictability* of their jobs. Their ability to fight fires is something that they often hang their hat on—but also something that, too often, makes *their day* feel like a complete dumpster fire. The only way they can "get it all done" with an already bursting calendar and an already full plate is by stretching work time into nights and weekends. That's why I recommend pre-planning time to fight the fires.

I know it sounds counterintuitive, but hear me out. Consider a day where you're stacked back-to-back until 5:30 p.m. with the exception of two breaks: one is thirty minutes you've snagged at 1:30 p.m. that you hope to use to grab (and somehow eat) lunch. The second is from 3:00–4:00 p.m. when you have "to-do list time."

But at 10:00 a.m., a fire lands on your desk, and now the whole day has to be rearranged. Lunch is now a Kind bar, and that's only because you had one in your drawer (so what if it's open, and the top is kind of stale—it's food!). Your to-do list time has been scheduled over by the 10:00 a.m. non-urgent (but still important) meeting you had to shift to deal with the morning fire. The day ends at 5:30 p.m., but you're hungry, and you have an email inbox you haven't looked at all day—not to mention the list you started the morning with.

After a string cheese (or perhaps going through the after-school-to-bedtime routine if you're a parent), you sit back down at your computer and finish up the last few hours of the day—gobbling up your evening and leaving you exhausted.

That's what's so powerful about creating the fire-fighting block proactively on your calendar. Consider the same scenario but with a fire-fighting block (past coaching clients have also named this a "flex block" like Danielle did, a "pivot block," or an "agility block") from 2:00–3:00 p.m.

Of course, you wouldn't say to your stakeholders, "Thanks for looping me in on this: I'd be happy to help in four hours when I get to my agility block!" Rather, you have a scenario where you can reschedule the morning meeting that got pushed without giving up lunch or that to-do list time. It creates a release valve on your calendar, enabling you to handle the fire without sending your whole day up in flames.

Planning time to firefight can't help us predict what the next fire will look like or where it will pop up. But it's just about the closest thing we can do to predict the unpredictable, and plan accordingly: allowing us to be impactful and responsive in a way that doesn't crush us.

> **#4. Avoid the "Yes… Damn!" Trap.** How many times have you said "yes" to something in the future because this week was busy, but your calendar had a lot more white space three weeks out? You say yes to the task force meeting or that going-away happy hour for the colleague you've barely ever spoken to… only to see it on your stacked-to-the-brim calendar three weeks later and say, "Damn! Why did I commit to that?" You either (a) cancel and feel bad because you're not being "productive" in following through on your commitments, (b) no-show and feel worse, or (c) attend and feel resentful.

That is the "Yes… Damn!" Trap. Coined by Yale School of Management's Dr. Gal Zauberman, it's a psychological phenomenon (also known as a "planning fallacy") in which we overestimate how available we'll be in the future. With our eyes bigger than our stomachs, we create a cycle where we're too often setting ourselves and others up for disappointment—overwhelming ourselves with an overabundance of commitments.

Our programming around productivity makes us want to say "yes" to doing everything, and we often convince ourselves the future will be less busy in order to make good on those productivity commitments. But research shows that the biggest statistical predictor of how busy we'll be in the future is how busy we are this week. So before you fall into the next "Yes... Damn!" Trap in your life, ask yourself this question: does this commitment serve my goals in a meaningful way?

#5. Choose What You Will "Fail" At. For so many of us, *Being Busy = Being Successful* and *Being Productive = Being Valuable*. But as we've established, that's just not true.

Still, making peace with not "doing it all" is hard—and that's exactly why Oliver Burkeman reminds us we must choose what to "fail at" when it comes time. As the author of *Four Thousand Weeks: Time Management for Mere Mortals* explains, our desire to win against the "dictatorship of the clock" inherently makes us a loser. "Time can't be mastered at all and we're wasting it [by trying]," he explains. "Getting comfortable with the discomfort of knowing that we can't win time helps us come to grips."

That's why Burkeman argues we must choose what we will "fail at" so that we can succeed at the things that matter most. For example, he reminds, "Mastering your email only makes you get more emails."

Think of this as putting your money where your mouth is on the "impactful vs. productive" mindset you may have adopted a few pages ago. I trust you to decide what you need to "fail at" or "let go of" in order to succeed at the things that matter most. The question is: do *you* trust you?

Our obsession with productivity isn't helping us master our time; it's gobbling it up. So why are we using our most precious and only non-renewable resource—one, Burkeman reminds us, that is continuously diminishing as we live each of the 4,000 weeks the average adult will have in a lifetime—working toward inbox zero? Dr. Whillans ups the ante, reminding us that "how we spend our time signals everything we care about in life."

That's why it's so urgent that we reclaim our time and protect it: reimagining how we want to use it each day, and reassessing our relationship to productivity in order to unhook from the rules of the Old Playbook that no longer serve us.

If reassessing your relationship with productivity and time feels radical, you're not doing it wrong. As Eve Rodsky, gender equity advocate and *New York Times* best-selling author of *Fair Play*, reminded at one of Adesiyan's events, "Being unavailable is revolutionary. It's an act of resistance."

This is something we'll explore further in our next chapter as we write the rules of the New Playbook together on boundaries.

CHAPTER 9:

BUILDING BOUNDARIES

———

"Randi, you look like shit."

This is how he greeted me when my former-boss-but-for-ever-mentor sat down for breakfast together on a crisp autumn morning.

Once upon a time, the spot we were sitting in was a decrepit parking lot where I used to catch the MegaBus to New York City for a buck. Now, it was a fancy shopping plaza where you could pick up an Hermés Birkin Bag on your lunch break or sip a seven-dollar cappuccino over a power breakfast, like we were doing.

Scheduled under the pretense of "catching up," my mentor had really asked me to breakfast to pitch me on a job: would I consider, he asked, coming to work for him again at a new start-up he'd just joined?

Just as quickly as our catch-up turned into a pitch, our pitch turned into an intervention: "No, really," he asked me. "What's going on? Because you seriously look like shit."

I couldn't fault him. I *did* look like shit, and I totally *felt* like shit. My hair was falling out of my head, I was losing weight, and my performance in my day-job was starting to slip for the first time ever in my career. Working at a different start-up, parenting two children under three, and running my coaching business in earnest part-time left me exhausted in a way that coffee—even if somebody could have hooked me up to an IV drip for it—just could not fix.

As our conversation progressed, I told him I appreciated the offer, but there was no way I could possibly come work for him; I was officially burned out on my career in business development.

"You're not burned out on sales. You're burned out on *life*," he challenged back. Then he said:

> *The way I see it, you have three really big things happening right now—you have this big business development job, you have two little kids, and you have a side hustle that seems to be much more than a 'little side hustle.'*
>
> *You need to choose two of those three things if you want to feel good—and we know you're not giving up your kids. We also know that you probably aren't giving up this business, and you shouldn't.*
>
> *If you decide you do want to give that up and double down on sales, you can come work for me anytime you want. But I don't think it's what you really want. Let's talk about what you need to do to quit your job and take this business full-time, and I will do everything in my power to support you.*

Six weeks later, I quit my job. I didn't feel totally "ready"— far from it. I didn't even have a fully formed business plan. I just knew that, while things looked great from the outside, I was totally and completely off the rails on the inside.

There were no boundaries anymore in my day or in my life. To make it all (barely) work, I worked constantly. I said yes to everything, not because I *wanted* to, but because I was terrified of saying no.

Instead of being honest with myself about what I could handle up until that point, for too long I had continued to justify it. I constantly steamrolled through my own boundaries, telling myself, *It's just this quarter at work... It's just this one deal... It's just this season of life with my kids.*

I had been doubling down on my boundary-busting habits to keep up the appearance of looking polished to the outside world. But he had caught me in my messiest moment and called me on it. I felt like I was going to crash at any moment.

OFF THE RAILS

If our careers are the track, it's critical to remember that our boundaries are the guardrails of our life. When we ignore them, we eventually go off the rails.

When we consider them intellectually, most of us feel really clear about our boundaries: what we absolutely will and won't accept. Yet sometimes, when we go to work, we're really quick to disregard them—especially when it comes to the boundaries that protect our time, bandwidth, and wellbeing.

Too often, we say yes to things that violate our boundaries when every warning sign inside of us is dying to say no. Sometimes those signs are physical. They can be as dramatic as what I was experiencing or as subtle as tightness in our chest, a pit in our stomach, holding our breath, or feeling our heart pound when a request lands in our inbox. As much as these you're-near-or-past-your-boundary signals can be physical, they can also be emotional: tears, fear, resentment, or racing thoughts that just won't stop.

So how do you know if you've gone off the rails? If you've ever said "yes" to something and found yourself immediately engulfed by a tidal wave of dread, you've gone off the rails. If you've ever done the verbal gymnastics of completely over-explaining or justifying a "no" to a client, colleague, or boss, you've gone off the rails.

THREE REASONS BRILLIANT WOMEN GO OFF THE RAILS

The Old Playbook taught us to constantly push harder, grind it out, and say yes to every opportunity... So let me ask you: how's that going for you?

I thought so.

The ironic thing about busting our own boundaries is that we often think it will allow us to move closer to goals when just the opposite is true. It's not a matter of "if" but "when" we will derail ourselves by burning out, jeopardizing our health, or simply coming to resent the things we were once passionate about at work. If this sounds familiar, you're not alone, and here are three common reasons I consistently see high-achieving women make bad boundary choices.

Off the Rails Bad Habit #1: We let insecurity masquerade as a "good choice." Sometimes we don't set a boundary and say yes to something even when we feel maxed out because we tell ourselves it's the "right thing to do." Or we feel like we're at capacity, and we're getting really close to that guardrail, but something "truly urgent" arises, and we "need" to deal with it. Or, perhaps, this is "the opportunity we have been waiting for" to get in front of the right people.

Being able to make those judgment calls is absolutely critical to our success, but it's also where we have the potential for major trouble. That happens when we let our insecurity masquerade as a "good choice."

Remember, our Inner Critics think *everything* that impacts the way people might see us is urgent—an impulse often fueled by our perfectionistic, overachieving, or external-validation-driven behaviors. As a result, our Inner Critics talk us into saying yes, rationalizing every reason why crossing this boundary *du jour* is just the "right call."

Really, we're saying yes because we're worried that by saying no, we'll be rejected, judged, or left out of the next opportunity. This insecurity can feel particularly acute if we work for somebody who doesn't seem to respect their own boundaries—or worse, somebody who doesn't respect ours when we set them.

Adding insult to injury, we often feel insecure about *being* insecure, which makes it even more tempting for us to rationalize those feelings away. In fact, according to Harvard's Dr. Ashley Whillans, one of the top reasons high-performing women are loath to say no, clarify expectations, or ask for help is because they fear being perceived as "lazy" by their colleagues. Our Inner Critics are habitual boundary crossers, and our lives go off the rails when we can't distinguish them from our Voice of Reason.

Off the Rails Bad Habit #2: We fear disappointing others more than we fear disappointing ourselves. For many of us, as we covered our *Ditching*

Perfectionism and *Untethering from External Validation* chapters, we have ingrained habits of prioritizing
other people's needs and perceptions over our own.
As a result, we tell ourselves a toxic story that disappointing others has a higher cost than disappointing
ourselves.

That's because it's a lot *easier* to disappoint ourselves than
it is to disappoint others.

We fear that the boss will remember this during the performance review or bonus season, or that they won't ask us to
take on that next leadership opportunity. We might also get
nervous that the disappointed client will move in a different
direction. The risk of disappointing ourselves seems to have
lower consequences when, actually, those consequences are
often higher—even if they're just more private.

When we disrespect our boundaries, the initial consequences are usually ones that only we can see or feel:
dread, sadness, frustration, exhaustion, or resentment. As
those build, they can escalate into more tangible consequences such as impaired judgment, anxiety, depression,
and burnout.

Worse, sometimes we actually have the audacity to *beat
ourselves up* for feeling that way in the first place, gaslighting
ourselves on why we're making this "more than it needs to
be." It's a vicious cycle we need to end. We can start by recognizing that we're most tempted to disrespect our own boundaries and go off the rails when we don't properly account for
the cost of disappointing ourselves.

**Off the Rails Bad Habit #3: We are rewarded for dis-
respecting our boundaries**. In my twenties, I worked

for a company with a pervasive culture of overwork. I loved so many things about the people and the experience, but norms inside our boundary-busting culture created the worst habits I'd ever learned at work. I wanted to say *no* to taking on one more client, *no* to one more trip, *no* to squeezing in one more phone call (often from airport lounges between connecting flights), so why did I say yes? And then continue to say yes for years after I left?

I was rewarded again and again by way of compensation, opportunities, exposure, and praise for habitually ignoring my boundaries.

Going off the rails didn't feel like I was plummeting in some dangerous free fall. It felt like it was my ticket to success—or at least a version of success defined by external validation from others around me. As I learned, however, you can only sustain that for so long. Success starts to feel hollow when you're so exhausted you can't even enjoy it. Even worse, one bad week, month, or quarter can suddenly feel like an existential personal failure when you've pinned everything you care about on how others perceive you.

By chance, my phone rang on one of those "I just can't do this for much longer" days while I was sitting on the couch in my room at the Westin Indianapolis Convention Center, a regular spot on my work travel circuit. It was a call about a job that I'd ultimately take and one that would totally change my life. Scared to leave the overwork job where I didn't have boundaries but had oodles of social capital and a clear career trajectory, I had already said "no" three times to the offer at the new company. Then, a few weeks later, they came back around, ultimately making me an offer I couldn't refuse. I walked into that job with a 100 percent salary increase and a 100 percent level of awareness that I just couldn't (nay, wouldn't) work like that again.

Until that point, I *thought* I was rewarded for disregarding my boundaries. As I would learn, those accolades were just consolation prizes. I was rewarded more handsomely than I could have ever imagined for finally standing up for them.

WHEN "NO" MAKES US STRONGER

"There's no question. No female gymnast in history has ever taken on this event like Simone Biles," the announcer whispered as Biles chalked her hands at the top of the vault's long blue runway at the Tokyo Games in the summer of 2021.

Kicking her foot to the side and wiping her hands, the camera zoomed in as she took a long inhale through her nose. The camera fixed on her face, she exhaled into a moment of utter stillness, and the camera zoomed back out just as the announcer whispered again, "It doesn't matter what vault she does. It's a show stopper, and it's must-see TV."

That's when Biles bounded down the runway, sprung over the vault, and uncharacteristically stumbled when she tried to stick the landing. Biles grimaced and walked right off the competition floor to the surprise of the announcer and millions of people watching the event unfold on television. Like a Greek Chorus for the worldwide audience, he stammered, "Wow, very uncharacteristic for Simone," barely containing his surprise.

A few minutes later, Biles returned to the floor but not to compete. With her leotard off and the US Women's Gymnastics team's white sweatsuit on, Biles sat on the sideline— offering no explanation as she cheered on her teammates for the remainder of the competition.

While the action in women's gymnastics was usually on the floor, that evening, it was at the post-competition press conference. "No injuries, thankfully," Biles explained a few hours later to what may have been the most-watched press conference of the Tokyo games. "And that's why I took a step back because I didn't want to do something silly out there and get injured."

It had been a "difficult Olympic games," she continued. Explaining that this was not about a physical injury but about mental health, she said, "There's a lot of different variables, and I think we're just a little bit too stressed out. But we should be out here having fun, and sometimes that's not the case... I just felt like it would be a little bit better to take a back seat to work on my mindfulness. I knew that the girls would do an absolutely great job, and I didn't want to risk the team and medal. They've worked way too hard for that."

The media ran wild with headlines about Biles prioritizing her mental health (which was absolutely true), but the story was reduced to a parable about self-care. In the process, the media missed perhaps the most important thing that hundreds of millions of women around the world were seeing. This wasn't just about self-care; it was about setting a boundary. It was about watching a woman who is (literally) at the top of her professional field, at the top of her personal game, not just saying "yes" to self-care but creating a boundary by saying "no" to the obstacles that prevented it.

Biles felt like she was off the rails and said to the world that she needed a "mental rest." No apologies and no promises of what came next—just a simple explanation of what happened on that vault and the decision to "take it from there."

WHEN "YES" HOLDS US BACK

Maggie wasn't an elite gymnast, but she was kind of the government equivalent. Coming off her stint as a presidential appointee at a prominent government agency, she took a few months off to make up for lost time: hanging out with her two young kids, renovating her home, and looking for the perfect job. She had nothing to prove to anybody and had earned the right to be choosy… you heard me say presidential appointee, right? Okay, just checking.

When she found it, she was thrilled. It was exactly the type of work she loved to do with a great boss and great compensation. Already joining the organization as a leader on her team, she had a clear path to a promotion, the budget to advance her projects, and, the cherry on top, prestigious appointments to chair positions inside some of the industry's most influential trade associations.

It sounded like a dream, but soon Maggie felt like she was caught inside a nightmare. She was supposed to be defining the priorities, spearheading the strategic partnerships, and assembling the teams to get after them. Instead, she was acting like an overworked waitress at a diner: constantly on her feet, running around, trying to take everybody's order, sending back the eggs that were overcooked or the bacon that wasn't crispy enough, and refilling cups of cold coffee.

Except in Maggie's case, in between conference calls to Asia, meeting with national coalition partners, and writing policy she hoped Congress would adopt as legislation, she was also doing mountains of office housework: sifting through hundreds of carpet samples for the new office and personally making travel arrangements to ensure the company's president would be picked up from the airport in the right type of SUV when they all arrived for an off-site meeting.

"How are you doing?" I asked her one afternoon when we got on the phone for a 2:30 p.m. coaching session.

"Well, I haven't eaten anything since a piece of chocolate around six this morning, so you know… just pretty busy," she laughed, her giggle quickly falling into frustrated silence and sadness.

Maggie was totally off the rails when it came to her boundaries. Instead of focusing on her priorities, she was playing whack-a-mole on everybody else's priorities. As a self-proclaimed "Type-A person," she was running herself ragged cleaning up the mess of a completely disorganized company culture. Without her boundaries at work, it felt more and more like her *whole life* was going off the rails— she was exhausted and constantly missing dinner to be on conference calls held across different time zones. She was resentful of the job she was once so excited about.

Worse, she was convinced that feeling off the rails at work meant something was wrong with her, not the company's reactive, tumultuous culture. After venting about another work week of whack-a-mole, she took a breath. "It's actually fine," she insisted. "I like a challenge, and I can handle this."

"This is not a challenge," I protested. "This is a struggle. A challenge levels you up, and a struggle just levels you. There is nothing about this situation that is leveling you up or moving you closer to your goals right now."

That was the turning point for Maggie. She was willing to handle a challenge—like a large portfolio of policy issues or an uphill battle with a Congressional Subcommittee. She was struggling, and it wasn't just impacting her. She felt like a shell of herself when she got home and had nothing left to give to her kids. She was declining invitations to the things she loved, like wine nights with her friends and golf dates with her husband.

A lack of boundaries wasn't just keeping her from the things she loved outside of work, they were also keeping her from the things she most enjoyed about her job. She did not care about carpet samples (seriously, she had renovated her house during her mini-sabbatical and did not need to do it again for somebody else).

So, slowly and with great trepidation, Maggie started setting boundaries. First, she tackled the complete chaos of her office culture. A self-described process-and-systems maven, instead of cleaning up each individual mess, she started identifying a new problem each week and bringing a *systems recommendation* to each leadership team meeting that the office could implement as a policy. This extricated her from the office housework, allowing her to clean up problems at scale and from a position of leadership—instead of walking around the office as a human Swiffer Sweeper.

Next, she sat her boss down to revisit her quarterly priorities. Handling the office move, she explained, was taking priority over the critical policy and coalition issues in her portfolio. In response, her boss promptly transferred this task to a colleague. He was less attentive to detail than she was, but that was his problem, not hers. It required setting a boundary with *herself* to not swoop in and constantly clean up his mess.

Lastly, instead of responding rapid-fire to every email that crossed her inbox, Maggie began asking herself questions instead of just firing back replies: Does this need a response *right now*? Does this need a response *from me*? How much will this matter six days, weeks, or months later? What's the trade-off if I say yes to this?

The world did not blow up. Quite the opposite, she was almost instantaneously commanding a new level of respect, clout, and control that was unimaginable just a few weeks prior. She thought that constantly saying yes put her in a position of power and control. It was only in saying no that she learned it was putting her in a 24/7 stress tizzy and, notably, a position of weakness.

She also learned that building and protecting her guardrails takes an extraordinary amount of practice—including some backsliding. Instead of beating herself up when it happened, we started getting curious: What did her Inner Critic believe about this? Where were her old habits around perfectionism and internal validation popping up? Understanding her motives was critical to changing her habits and managing the response when she backslid from time to time (because she's human) on choices she regretted. As Maggie learned, setting boundaries can be challenging. But it can also be life-changing.

THE NEW PLAYBOOK FOR
BUILDING YOUR BOUNDARIES

I know this is the part where you're looking for tips, but let me tell you about my short-lived professional football career first.

It was an unseasonably cold spring day in 2022 when I squared off against the NFL's Carolina Panthers. We were not on the football field but inside the Four Seasons Hotel & Spa Georgetown in Washington, DC.

I arrived that morning for my annual *Something Major Realign & Recharge Retreat*. With a coffee in one hand and a clipboard in another, I started a final walkthrough. But when I walked into the room where we'd be hosting an afternoon yoga class, I found a man who stood six foot three and rocked a bushy red beard. He was just standing there in a Carolina Panthers jacket with his arms crossed, making the kind of pouty face my then-three-year-old gave me when I told him he could only have one cookie, not two.

"Excuse me, sir," I said perkily (two coffees in) as I strode over to him in my signature leopard-print bomber jacket, "this space is closed for a private event today." He was, I assumed, totally lost. Why else would he be standing in the middle of a room set up for a yoga class at eight in the morning?

"Well, I'm with the Panthers, and this is my training room for the day," he told me. Still assuming there had been some confusion, I looked back up at him and smiled again. From the outside, we were like David and Goliath, but I was completely in control.

I was not going to be steamrolled just because he looked like Tormund from *Game of Thrones* or because he physically towered over me. I *maybe* cleared five foot three that day—and that was only because I had the added quarter-inch courtesy of the pink "Air" bubble on my tie-dye Nike Air Max sneakers.

But I was not going to be intimidated. I was going to be polite. "You must be confused," I repeated, smiling bigger this time. "This room is closed for a private event today."

"This is my room," he groused back, refusing to leave. Once again, reminding me of the toddler I had left at home thirty minutes before.

Still smiling and still perky, I channeled my inner toddler mom and said, "Yes, and this room is contractually obligated to me today until 5:00 p.m., so let's go find a member of the hotel's staff and figure this out together?" I was tempted to add an "okay, buddy?" the way I would talk to my son Theo, but instead gestured with my hands toward the door, inviting him to walk with me.

Still sulking and hulking around, he started to pitch a fit to the hotel staff—now T-minus twenty-five minutes before my guests were set to arrive. In an effort to appease our football friend, a staffer asked if we would consider giving the Panthers our room at 2:00 p.m. instead of 5:00 p.m., as we'd be out of that particular space by 1:00 p.m.

I was about to acquiesce, simply because I was busy and wanted the conversation to be over so I could finish up, when I remembered, "This is *my* room that I *paid* for." I wanted the women attending to be able to leave their belongings wherever they wanted and not worry about any noise they might make while we were next door doing our post-yoga lunch and wine-tasting. "No," I simply told them, and as I stuck my ground, he pouted off.

Completely coincidentally, boundaries were a topic of that retreat. So a few hours later, when discussing my tools for designing and reinforcing your guardrails, I went completely off-script. Ditching my prepared talking points, I told them this same story. That boundary crosser could have ruined my day and the day of everybody else who had joined. Instead, he was new material for illustrating three of my favorite boundaries tools:

1. "No" is a complete sentence.
2. Say "no" by embracing the Golden Rule of Improv: "yes... and."
3. Rethink the cost calculus.

Let's break them down—plus discuss a fourth bonus tool for when your boss is *still* a habitual boundary-buster—so that you have them in your back pocket the next time you square off against the Carolina Panthers in your own life.

#1. No is a Complete Sentence. At their essence, our boundaries are what we're willing to accept from other people and what we're willing to accept from ourselves. That's why having permission to say "no" isn't just okay—it's vital, it's existential, and it's your agency. As Eve Rodsky explains in her book *Unicorn Space: Reclaim Your Creative Life in a Too-Busy World*, "It's time to give yourself permission to be unavailable. You are complicit in your own oppression when you willingly put yourself and your time second or last."

You have permission to say no to things. Full stop.

Consider this: if you keep saying yes to things that violate your boundaries, are you going to climb to the top or burn out? Are you actually going to execute with excellence or will your work suffer? The Old Playbook taught us to always keep pushing, and yet, there aren't enough of us in leadership. We're actively backsliding in terms of women's earnings and representation in the workforce, and we're notching record highs for women's burnout and record lows for women's happiness.

Never forget that you have permission to use no as a complete sentence. Also, know that this is a skill you'll have to develop. So start practicing getting more comfortable in low-stakes environments so you have the experience, confidence, and muscle memory to start using it when the stakes are high.

#2. Channel Your Inner Tina Fey with "Yes... And."
I appreciate that learning to say "no" can be hard. That is why one of my favorite ways to say "no" is by channeling my inner Tina Fey, the hilarious comedian and SNL legend, and borrowing one of the golden rules of improv comedy: saying "yes... and."

Colette Gregory, a mental-health-counselor turned improv-comedian who performs with the renowned Second City improv troupe where Fey cut her teeth, explains, "In improv, 'yes... and' is our cornerstone philosophy. The 'yes' means we accept whatever our scene partner says to us while the 'and' allows us to build on whatever that statement is to create the scene together."

Importantly, Gregory clarifies, "When we come from a place of yes, that looks like every idea is being celebrated—even if we aren't agreeing with it." That's exactly why it can be key to collaboratively setting a boundary, while "reinforcing partnership and psychological safety in the process."

I've watched countless clients use "yes... and" to set boundaries accordingly, and here are a few examples.

"Yes, I'd be happy to help with that, *and* I will be able to turn to that next week."

"Yes, I'd love to set up some time to discuss this idea, *and* let's also carve out some time in that conversation to talk about adjustments we'll need to make to team bandwidth, projects, and structure if this is going to be a priority this quarter."

I've also seen clients use "yes... and" to set boundaries at home with statements like, "Yes, I'm excited to come for Christmas, *and* we'll be coming from Christmas Eve to Boxing Day, then taking our own vacation time through New

Year's," or, "Yes, I can plan to cook dinner, *and* that means I'll need your help to pick the kids up from soccer."

When you're dying to say "no" but feel like you can't, turn to "yes... and" instead to collaboratively co-design your boundaries with your stakeholders.

> **#3. Rethink the Cost Calculus.** We are often quick to overestimate the cost of saying no to something or someone (e.g., fear of rejection, perceived consequences of disappointing others) and *equally* quick to overestimate the benefits of saying yes (e.g., the fleeting joy of external validation). So before you react by instantaneously replying to the request and blurting "yes" to something, take time to rethink the cost calculus.

Instead of just evaluating the cost of *setting* the boundary, ask yourself: what is the cost of *not setting* the boundary?

Over the years, I've watched the costs add up as follows: feeling exhausted all the time, saying yes to something only to perform sub-optimally on it (which looks so much worse than setting the boundary in the first place), or resentment toward the work that has led them to burnout and quitting.

On the flipside, here are some of the benefits I've observed for the women who *did* rethink the cost calculus and set boundaries: seeing a situation resolve itself before their rapid-fire email response came back, better performance (as reflected by successful work outcomes, positive performance reviews, promotions, or raises), increased fulfillment at work, increased creativity, and a decrease of people dumping needless work/office housework on their plate. Taking time to rethink the cost calculus gives you space to slow down, think through the scenarios, and even check your Inner Critic (who is likely to catastrophize the cost of setting a boundary) in the process.

#4. Make a Plan for Managing Boundary-Busting Bosses. Sometimes we can set up all the guardrails in the world, but a habitually boundary-busting boss will come and plow right through them. That's why it's critical to have a plan to handle the three most common types of boundary-busting bosses. My friend and mentor Mary Abbajay wrote the book on managing up (no, really, it's actually called *Managing Up*), and she shares some of her best tips for the three most common offenders.

- **The Workaholic:** While your boss may be happy to grind it out 24/7, you don't have to. If you've had a clear conversation about your boundaries—a must, Abbajay reminds—and emails continue to come in on nights and weekends, "Don't just *assume* that they expect you to answer every email. Make sure they understand how amazing your output is and look for strategic above-and-beyond moments to go the extra mile when a big project or high-profile priority crosses your desk."

- **The Repeat Offender:** Abbajay reminds that it's often our actions—not our words—that reinforce boundaries, "If that email comes in at 8:00 p.m., and it's not urgent, think 'show, don't tell.' You can simply ignore it and handle it in the morning. Our actions sometimes speak louder than words."

- **The Toxic Boss:** "Whether your boss is a screamer, shouter, narcissist, bully, or gaslighter, when it comes to a toxic boss you cannot set enough boundaries to thrive. You can only set boundaries to survive until you can get out," Abbajay explains. "Study after study shows us that the best thing we can do with a truly toxic boss is to get out." In the meantime, Abbajay suggests prioritizing your mental health, focusing on the quality of your work product, reducing one-on-one interactions where the worst behavior may occur, and keeping as much communication documented as possible.

"Boundaries are loving. They make us feel safe," explained author and child psychologist, Claire Lerner. Speaking totally off-the-cuff in the Q&A of one of our Something Major working moms events, you could have heard a pin drop in the room. While the answer came in response to a mom's question about a power struggle with her kids, Claire's words hit every woman in that room like a ton of bricks. There's a reason why they're important to kids, and that's exactly the reason they're just as important to adults: boundaries *are* loving, and they *do* make us feel safe.

It's something Biles echoed when she pulled out of the competition in Tokyo, reminding us that boundaries are a source of strength, not weakness. We *must* put ourselves first so we can perform at our best. If we don't, she implores, "You're not going to succeed as much as you want to. It's okay sometimes to even sit off the big competitions to focus on yourself because it shows how strong of a competitor you really are, rather than just battling through it."

Our boundaries aren't obstacles that prevent us from achieving the pinnacle of our careers. They're the guardrails that allow us to get there. Guardrails keep us from crashing our cars, and they can keep us from crashing our careers, our dreams, and our sanity, too. Taking care of ourselves is critical to our success. Boundaries are just one side of the coin; think of them as the defense. The other side of that coin is actively investing in our wellbeing and rethinking our self-care. We'll discuss how to go on the offense in our final chapter, *Reimagining Wellbeing*.

CHAPTER 10:

REIMAGINING WELLBEING

I want to talk to you about a subject that is probably going to make you uncomfortable and bring up some unpleasant memories… and that is diarrhea.

But before we get there, let me tell you about a brilliant financier I coached named Ling.

Ling wasn't just good at her job. She was *excellent* at her job, and she gave it everything she had. Literally, everything.

To do that, she made some big sacrifices along the way. This included letting go of a relationship with the partner that she "probably should have married" when she departed one global finance hub to take a "career-making" opportunity in another one—an entire continent away.

She also made small daily and weekly sacrifices—at least, she thought they were small—including "every ounce" of her free time. That meant giving up dating, frequently canceling dinner with friends, and postponing cherished time with her family.

On paper, it paid off. When she hired me to coach her, she was on the cusp of a major promotion at one of the world's most prestigious firms. The magnitude of this opportunity was not lost on her, especially as a woman of color in a very white, very male industry.

Ling was a total superstar, and with that major promotion on the horizon, she was pushing herself harder than ever. In classic Performative Productivity Culture fashion, she felt like self-care could wait and boundaries could be formed on the other side of scoring this huge promotion. Taking time for herself "just wasn't worth it." Even a would-be-relaxing, off-the-grid camping trip was completely derailed by her constant quest to find cell service in the woods to check on deals.

While I was challenging Ling on her priorities (when we started, she went out of her way to tell me how important the things she routinely moved to the backburner were to her, like dating and family time), after the camping trip, I moved from concerned to alarmed. I told her I was worried she was going to burn out—and pass out right before the finish line of the marathon she had been running for years—if she couldn't start making self-care a bigger part of her routine. "I want to support your goals," I told her. "What do you think about working on this together?"

But Ling rebuffed me, telling me that, "Self-care is for other people in less demanding jobs." Plus, she *was* practicing self-care, she insisted. Her definition of self-care was scrolling email from bed in the morning (instead of at her desk) and hitting the gym for thirty minutes before work (on the mornings when overnight emails from the world's other banking hubs didn't keep her from the treadmill, of course).

There was no doubt in my mind that Ling loved her job and that she was excellent at it—and that was *exactly* why I was so concerned. So when we got on the phone one afternoon, and she cried telling me she was so exhausted that it hurt, I knew we had a full-blown crisis on our hands—*and* an opportunity.

As one of my mentors, Ken Mossman, says, "Tears aren't good or bad. They just tell us something important is here with us in the conversation right now." And something *was* important here. Ling had hit her breaking point. After crying for a few minutes, she blew her nose, wiped her tears, and told me she had to "pull it together." She had three Zoom calls after our coaching session that she "needed to attend," and she just had to "get through the day." Plus, she couldn't be blotchy on her next call.

"How?" I asked tenderly, working to self-manage my concern and meet her where she was.

Dodging my question and insisting that she "absolutely, positively could not miss" them, I went for a Hail Mary and blurted, "But what if you had diarrhea?"

"What?" she exclaimed at me—and even though we were on the phone, I could feel her practically fall out of her seat.

"Seriously," I doubled down, "imagine you had awful, terrible, crampy, explosive diarrhea. Are you telling me you would seriously bring your laptop into your bathroom and Zoom from your toilet?"

What Ling had is the emotional equivalent of diarrhea: a stop-your-world, put-life-on-hold until this passes moment. In fact, Ling is not an exception. Too often, she is the rule: proof of the sacrifice-it-all, work-ourselves-'til-burnout, self-care-is-weakness culture we live in. She scored her promotion after all, but not without a cost. In the swirl of her stress, she could only see two options—carry on as-is or quit.

Here's the honest truth we need to talk about when we talk about reimagining wellbeing: sometimes we muscle through and *do* get everything we (think) we want—but at what cost? Other times, on the way to getting there, we "girl boss too close to the sun" like Liz from our *Reassessing Productivity and Reclaiming Time* chapter and get burned (or just burned out). Just because we *can* get through doesn't mean we always want to—or that we actually enjoy the day-to-day of our lives when everything is perfect on paper (or our LinkedIn profile), but we're silently dying inside.

Like too many women I speak with daily, Ling made it to the top but was one bad day, one bad email, one bad project, or one bad deal away from making that second choice. Unsurprisingly, I've had countless women tell me that they see themselves in Ling's story. They're convinced they "can't change anything" because their work is too demanding, or this season is too busy—pushing themselves until the situation unravels into a complete crisis.

Sometimes, that crisis is one of fulfillment. You claw your way to the top of the mountain, muscle through your exhaustion, and ditch all non-professional priorities only to get to the top of the hill and realize you don't even like the view. Worse, sometimes that crisis is one of complete burnout, and I've watched too many women tell me they "can't change anything" only to quit their job a matter of months or years later.

WELLBEING BASICS: UNDERSTANDING SELF-CARE, STRESS, BURNOUT, AND EXHAUSTION

The Old Playbook taught us to focus exclusively on working hard and doing whatever it takes to get the job done. With women unhappy, burned out, and leaving the workforce in record numbers, we must acknowledge that this just isn't working. That's why wellbeing isn't a nice-to-have in the New

Playbook. It's table stakes. So let's get on the same page about the basics of wellbeing and define three key terms we throw around casually.

- **Exhaustion:** Ling was experiencing what Dr. Christina Maslach describes as classic "exhaustion." A professor of psychology at the University of California Berkeley who pioneered the study of burnout, Dr. Maslach explains, "We will see people who have exhaustion, because they have way too much to do and can't possibly meet all the demands... But they still like their job and they feel good about what they're doing." That continuous pushing through the chronic exhaustion may get us to the next quarter, project, or promotion, but it puts us at high risk for burnout.

- **Stress:** Notably, exhaustion is different from regular old stress—my favorite definition of which is the "psychological perception of pressure."

- **Burnout:** Together, Dr. Maslach explains, continuous stress coupled with chronic exhaustion starts to make us feel cynical and ultimately burned out. In fact, burnout is what happens when we redirect the stress and exhaustion we feel about the *job* inwards—toward *ourselves*. When we're in a state of burnout, we often get cynical about our jobs, companies, industries *and* about our own lives. This leads us to start second-guessing our abilities and our decisions. That cycle of cynicism, exhaustion, and negativity begins to function like a riptide, threatening to drown us as we swim against the current.

To understand how we *personally* experience exhaustion, burnout, and stress, we also have to zoom out: Dr. Maslach notes that we have to look out for patterns where "job stressors" (like hours, expectations, deadlines, or culture) are both frequent and chronic. When they are, that's a red flag that the problem is one that might transcend the individual—requiring change across the unit, team, workgroup, organization, or even occupation.

Wellbeing is even bigger than industry or occupation. It transcends the very structure of our society and starts with systemic bias. One example is explored in research from Harvard's T.H. Chan School of Public Health that shows that racism negatively impacts health. We'd be missing a critical part of this conversation if we didn't look at the way structural bias taxes women's wellbeing.

With all that in mind, how could we ever possibly say that self-care has to wait? It might be one of the most important tools in the New Playbook, and I want to be clear about creating a shared definition for it here:

- **Flourishing vs. Functioning:** Self-care is not simply going out for manicures and massages (though they can be fabulous). It's the act of nourishing ourselves so we can flourish, not simply function, and that distinction is critical. Self-care should (1) actively recharge and re-energize you, (2) inspire calm, joy, creativity, or contentment, and (3) unlock the best version of yourself. That's why it's not enough for our self-care to be reactive. *Proactive* self-care is essential to our wellbeing, and there are many ways to cultivate it.

- **The Four Pillars of Self-Care**: These are comprised of the physical, emotional, intellectual, and spiritual. While there is no right or wrong way to practice self-care (for example, introverts recharge best quietly and alone, while extroverts recharge most effectively by connecting with others), below is a breakdown of common activities inside each of the four pillars.

Physical	Emotional
Taking care of our bodies:	*Taking care of our feelings:*
• Sleeping well • Getting proper nourishment • Exercising • Getting fresh air	• Connecting with a loved one • Quiet/alone time • Going screen-free • Limiting news and social media
Intellectual	**Spiritual**
Using our brains outside of work:	*Connecting to something greater:*
• Reading • Learning • Creating • Playing/listening to music	• Practicing mindfulness • Practicing meditation • Organized religion • Connecting with nature

FACT AND FICTION: THE FIVE SELF-CARE MYTHS

Over the years, I have observed an alarming trend that is holding high-performing women back: we get trapped inside one of The Five Self-Care Myths. Which one is your self-care kryptonite?

Self-Care Myth #1: The Myth of Indulgence. Like Ling said, "Self-care is a *luxurious indulgence* I just don't have time for, or it should be saved for a special occasion like a spa day or a vacation."

Self-Care Myth #2: The Myth of Self-Discipline. Here's how Maggie, the former presidential appointee and public policy maven we met in the last chapter, put it: "If I was just disciplined enough with my time or worked harder at the things on my to-do list, I'd have this time for myself. I don't need to do self-care right now. I need to work more and change my habits to earn it in the future."

Self-Care Myth #3: The Myth of It's Just This Season of Life. Here's how Alyssa, a manager for a global e-commerce platform, described it to me: "The issue isn't my self-care. It's just the season of life I'm in. We have a lot going on, and I just need to get through so that I can enjoy what's on the other side. This is just temporary."

Self-Care Myth #4: The Myth of I Should Be Grateful. This is how Zoe, an entertainment executive, described it to me: "When I stop and think about it, so many people have it so much harder than I do. I shouldn't complain about how tired or stressed I feel. I should be grateful for what I have."

Self-Care Myth #5: The Myth of Maintenance *Is* Self-Care: Finally, here's how Jess, a fundraiser, described it to me: "No, I *do* do self-care. I do self-care by having some quiet time to go to Target by myself or listening to podcasts while I fold laundry and cook dinner."

Do any of these sound familiar? In my experience, most women see themselves inside one (or multiple) of these stories—and it's the thing standing between you and your wellbeing. As psychiatrist Dr. Melissa Welby notes, "self care isn't rocket science," but it's still so hard sometimes.

FACT VS. FICTION: OUR SELF-CARE TRUTHS

From getting sleep and eating healthy, to making time for fun, Dr. Welby reminds us that self-care constitutes the most basic activities we can prioritize "to help you balance stress and optimize your life." We are all smart women, so let's heed Welby's reminder that this is not rocket science and start making better choices. Below are the Three Self-Care Truths that can help you unlock your wellbeing, leadership, and longevity.

#1. Self-care isn't an indulgence; it's a conduit to our performance. This is perhaps the most basic of all the Self-Care Truths yet something high-performing women continuously deny themselves. We are constantly pushing ourselves harder and raising the standards of what we expect from ourselves while lowering how we'll take care of ourselves to achieve them.

When it comes to anything else in our lives, we recognize this is common sense. In fact, it's just *physics*: matter doesn't move without energy.

Think about a race car. If the gas tank is empty, it cannot go 200 miles per hour no matter how much you want it to move forward, shame it to move forward, or punish it for not moving forward. So why are we any different? Seriously, I want you racing to your goals—not waiting on the side of the highway for AAA roadside assistance because you thought you could push through the blinking of the "tank empty" sign.

> **#2. Feelings have permission to co-exist.** You can feel tired, stressed, exhausted, or long for relaxation, *and* people can have it harder than you. You can feel grateful for your life *and* crave restoration and self-care. You have permission to let these things co-exist, not conflict. Full stop. We must stop weaponizing our gratitude as something we use to bully ourselves instead of appreciating our lives and cultivating opportunities to live fully into them.

> **#3. Errands are not self-care.** This one can get a little "spicy" as one of my former women's leadership cohort participants, Becky, so perfectly put it one year. Let me be clear: errands can be enjoyable, but they are not self-care, and we must avoid falling into the self-care trap of letting life's most basic maintenance activities qualify as your self-care.

Seriously, this is the equivalent of getting into your car on a sweltering summer day and saying, "You know what? I'm going to treat myself to air conditioning today." It's wonderful if life-maintenance activities are fun and contenting, but remember that self-care is about elevating us to flourishing, not just functioning. Listen, bonus points to you if your functioning activities can be done with pleasure—but that's *not* self-care in and of itself.

By June of 2020, I thought I had my pandemic exhaustion under control. I was dead wrong. I fell asleep at the wheel while driving my car through one of the biggest intersections in Washington, DC. I woke up to blaring horns from the few other cars that were on the road—who thankfully dodged me—only after I had already crossed six lanes of traffic, including a highway on-ramp. Miraculously, not a single person or car was hit, but I still shudder to think about what could have happened.

You might be waiting for me to say this was some kind of huge wake-up call (and it was). But if you're looking for me to tell you that I miraculously changed everything overnight, you'll be sorely disappointed.

The habits too many of us have around our boundaries and hustle culture are deeply ingrained. Slowing down takes work. As I learned that day, denying our wellbeing is not a nice-to-have. It's a need-to-have, and it may actually be the only thing in our work lives that is truly life or death. Here are five things I've learned about exhaustion and wellbeing since that moment that are essential to writing our New Playbook:

- **Operating exhausted at work is like driving drunk.** This is not a metaphor; this is science. Research from Harvard Medical School demonstrated that showing up to work exhausted has the equivalent cognitive impairment as showing up with a blood alcohol level about the legal limit to drive. If you wouldn't show up to your next Zoom meeting intoxicated, why is it okay to show up exhausted? We all know to not drink and drive, so now let's create a new rule: let's not sleep-deprive our-selves and expect our best work.

- **Most women feel like they're doing something wrong for being tired.** Research shows that it's often fear and shame that stop women from prioritizing self-care. According to Harvard's Dr. Ashley Whillans, who we met in our *Reassessing Productivity and Reclaiming Time* chapter, women are often hesitant to ask for help or seek solutions for taking something off their plate for fear of being perceived as lazy. Instead of asking for help, we get trapped in the shame spiral of *desiring support* in the first place and then hiding it. Unsurprisingly, research from LinkedIn showed that 62 percent of women surveyed in 2020 said they have downplayed their work, stress, or exhaustion for fear of retribution at work.

- **Even thirty seconds of self-care can make a measurable difference.** Research shows that even thirty second "micro-moments" of self-care can make a macro impact. Looking for a group of professionals whose time was measured solely by how they use time, researchers studied a group of call center workers. They assessed three key performance indicators (KPIs) and noted that those who took thirty-second micro-moments of self-care before each call outperformed their peers in productivity (it's counter-intuitive, but those who took small breaks had the best performance, as measured by the highest number of completed calls), work quality (they had the highest customer satisfaction scores), and a sense of fulfillment (they reported the highest job satisfaction scores). According to Dr. Whillans, who discussed the data on the *Harvard Business Review: Women at Work* podcast, the call center employees remind us that even in rigid work environments, "It's about spending the minutes, moments, hours and days of your life in a way that's consistent with the things and people you care about."

- **Dreams may be the brain's version of "active recovery" time.** New research shows that we need to rethink the idea that sleep is simply rest. Instead, psychologist and TED speaker Dr. Dylan Selterman likens dreams to taking an active recovery after physical exercise: "Whenever I'm doing a workout, and the person leading the workout says, 'Remember to do active recovery stretch, hydrate, and make sure you're doing the things that are essentially helping that rest and recovery process,' it's never sitting back, doing nothing." The same goes, he explains, for our dreams: sleep is like that active recovery for our brain, and when we dream, our brains are processing profound amounts of information—figuring out what is relevant and how we need to hold onto it, before "throwing out the rest" of that information. According to the Sleep Foundation, with over a third of Americans not getting enough sleep, and women habitually getting lower-quality sleep than men, it's critical that we rethink our relationship to rest.

- **Exercise is... complicated.** As *Let's Get Physical: How Women Discovered Exercise and Reshaped the World* author Danielle Friedman notes, "women's fitness culture is far from universally empowering... [it] is deeply intertwined with beauty culture, which sells the idea that women must change to be lovable—or even acceptable. Over the decades, fitness purveyors promising to lift women up have instead held them back and held them down by exploiting their insecurities." That's why it's so important that, as women, we evaluate what parts of our exercise routine nourish and uplift us, and which parts are acts of policing or judging our bodies. The latter is not self-care, and it's more urgent than ever as an estimated 75 percent of American women struggle with disordered eating, an important benchmark for measuring body positivity and confidence.

WELLBEING AS THE ENGINE OF SUCCESS, NOT A SPEED BUMP

"I just want to enjoy living," is all Nneka Chiazor could think as she woke up in the hospital bed, hooked up to tubes and machines.

Today, as Vice President of Public & Government Affairs at Cox Communications, Nneka is one of the country's most influential women in telecommunications policy. At the time, however, she was a new mom who had been laid off from work just days before delivering her first daughter—and she had just woken up from a coma.

Nine months pregnant and suddenly unemployed, Nneka sprinted into survival mode—or what she thought was survival mode. She spent the final days of her pregnancy feverishly updating her résumé, applying for jobs, and finishing the nursery—not wanting to miss a beat before she gave birth.

About a week after she gave birth, something just didn't feel right: "The last thing I remember is saying, 'This headache is so much for me. If I've got to go, I'm ready to go now.'"

In her haste to take care of everything and everyone besides herself, Nneka had silently been suffering through a life-threatening condition called eclampsia: "I was not taking care of myself. Period. I was taking care of projects at work, then looking for a new job. I was taking care of the nursery, the baby registry, and nesting. Sure, I was going to my doctor's visits, but I wasn't really taking care of myself."

Like so many other women who have white-knuckled through our never-ending list of to-do's (myself included), Nneka *thought* she had her priorities right. "Denying ourselves self-care is a social construct," Nneka reminds. "We're told to grin and bear it, to smile, that it's not that bad, that we all have a cape, and it must be flying at all times."

Then there's the social pressure, she adds, describing how she used to view self-care: "When I look around and see everyone is flying *their* cape all the time, why would I put mine down?"

The episode was a "wake-up call" that radically changed Nneka's perspective on self-care. But old habits die hard, and it wasn't as simple as flipping a switch. "'I haven't reached the pinnacle of self-care. It's a *practice*," she insists. "Self-care is that practice of listening to yourself, nourishing your soul, and understanding that it's okay to drop the superhero cape—and it's not selfish."

Discharged from the hospital to reunite with her daughter—and with a new lease on life—Nneka started, well, "enjoying living." She put a pause on her job search and started reveling in the small pleasures: traveling with her mother to Nigeria, taking up sewing classes, and watching Oprah.

Nneka hadn't taken a break from her professional relationships (she kept in touch), but she had taken a break from the hustle of it all—and she was rewarded. Around her daughter's first birthday, a job opportunity fell into her lap to become a project manager for the very client she was working with when she had been let go. From taking her blood pressure medication daily and finding doctors that made her feel heard to taking jazzercise ("that one will date me"), Nneka made self-care a top priority when she returned to work full-time.

By chance, she got staffed on a project for something called "FiOS," and her telecom career was born. As Nneka got busier, her self-care routine only became more regimented, adding things like no-meeting Fridays, regular PTO, quarterly massages, and a yearly international vacation.

Self-care hasn't been a speed bump in her career. It's been the engine sustaining her in a job where the only thing that is predictable is that something unpredictable is going to happen: "I recognize that, in this role, I have to be my authentic self to be authentic for the people I lead." She can only handle the phone call from the board member, the service issue with the client, and the question from her team all within the span of fifteen minutes *because* of her commitment to self-care.

It's the key, she insists, to accessing that authenticity within herself so she can share it with others. There are too many moving pieces, too many variables, and too many demands to *not* care for herself, she explains, and she expects the same from her team:

Self-care is loving myself, and it's my job to walk the walk. It's about modeling behavior. My team knows that when I am on vacation that I am on vacation. They're the subject matter experts, and it's my job to trust them to lead. When they are on vacation, if they check emails—if they even dare respond to an email—they get dinged. I have dollar fines that I'm putting on, and I'm not playing.

Attitudes about self-care are contagious in the workplace, which is why Nneka makes communication about self-care a priority for the team—whether that's stopping everything to hold a wellness meeting like she did following the January 6th insurrection, explicitly telling her team which company benefits she uses for mental wellness, or putting her doctor and dentist appointments on the calendar. Of all the tools Nneka practices and models, I asked her which was her biggest life hack:

Aside from choosing doctors I love, it's all about relationships. I shall not do toxic relationships. I will not be somebody else's emotional punching bag.

You've got to surround yourself with positive, caring, loving people—people who will be honest with you and not try to tear you down. If you don't have the right people in your corner, you don't have that wind beneath your wings. I've seen it, and I've experienced it. Positive relationships are a huge part of self-care because we don't live in isolation.

To that point, many of us get into bad self-care habits because other people around us have them. In the next section, we'll discuss how to shift *your* own habits and reimagine your relationship to your wellbeing.

THE NEW PLAYBOOK FOR REIMAGINING WELLBEING

While we have a long way to go in shifting the macroculture we work in, here are six tools from the New Playbook that will help shift your microculture: your personal relationship with wellbeing.

#1. Bust Your Self-Care Myths. One of the most important elements of redesigning your relationship with your wellbeing is understanding which one of these five is your personal kryptonite:

- Self-Care Myth #1: The Myth of Indulgence

- Self-Care Myth #2: The Myth of Self-Discipline

- Self-Care Myth #3: The Myth of It's Just This Season of Life

- Self-Care Myth #4: The Myth of I Should be Grateful

- Self-Care Myth #5: The Myth of Maintenance *is* Self-care

Take a moment and consider which one(s) you see yourself in. Then consider some of the following reflection questions, journaling your responses below.

- How does this self-care myth impact your wellbeing inside and outside of work?

- How does it impact your feelings about your career longevity?
- What are the costs and rewards of this myth in your life?
- What does your Inner Critic believe about this myth?
- When was a time in your life you neglected self-care, and what was the impact?

Understanding how this Self-Care Myth impacts you is key to rewriting the story on your own wellbeing. Now that you understand more about the impact, think back to the Self-Care Truths—#1. Self-care isn't an indulgence; it's a conduit to our performance, #2. Feelings have permission to co-exist, and #3. Errands are not self-care—and consider which could offer you a different path forward.

#2. Get Real on Self-Care "Guilt." Too often, I hear women tell me they feel "guilty" about taking the time they need to practice self-care when, really, they are *scared* of what other people will think of them when they take the time they need. To be clear, these are two different things.

Worrying about what other people will think of you isn't "guilt." It's being tethered to external validation and the need for others to approve of your decisions. Let's break it down:

- *Guilt* is what happens when we make a decision that *we* don't feel good about, usually because we have violated our personal code of conduct or values.
- *External validation* is the name of the game when we're worried about what *other people* will think of us. Or

when we worry about what others will say about us if we work less, do less, or say no to something to take the time we need for ourselves.

If what you're feeling is true "guilt" about your self-care time, then let's brainstorm different self-care activities below in our next tool. If what you're feeling is a fear of disappointing others or judgment from others for taking the time you need to focus on your wellbeing, then it's time to revisit your strategies about untethering from external validation. Like we discussed in our *Building Boundaries* chapter, remember that too often we fear disappointing others more than we fear disappointing ourselves. Your self-care *is* your career longevity and your personal fulfillment, so don't let yourself down.

#3. Build Your Personal Self-Care Tool Kit. As we discussed, there are four pillars of self-care—physical, emotional, intellectual, and spiritual. Using the visual of the four pillars we referenced earlier in the chapter, take out a journal and a pen. Inventory the things you're (a) already doing in each category, (b) feel aspirational about in each category (e.g., "I've never been into yoga, but I'd be willing to give it another try"), or (c) just curious to learn more about in each category. Pro tip: you can also download a printable copy of this chart at www.somethingmajorcoaching.com/book.

Physical	Emotional
Taking care of our bodies	*Taking care of our feelings*
Intellectual	**Spiritual**
Using our brains outside of work	*Connecting to something greater*

Remember, as Dr. Welby says, this is not rocket science, so start with the basic stuff, and celebrate the wins (woohoo!) for things you're already doing. We always get further when we go from strength to strength. So instead of obsessing over weaknesses and gaps, think about how you can build on those small wins. At the same time, pay attention to the categories that feel hard or weird, and give yourself permission to hang out there.

As Abraham Joshua Heschel, one of the leading Jewish theologians and philosophers of the twentieth century, notes, "Knowledge is fostered by curiosity; wisdom is fostered by awe."

There are so many answers in your self-care tool kit if you give yourself permission to ask yourself the questions about what's possible. Figuring out what self-care looks like for you might take curiosity and a willingness to explore the edges of what you thought possible. You don't have to commit to any outcomes, but promise you'll stay open to the process?

#4. Make a Plan. You've got your toolkit above? Or at least a few ideas scribbled down or bopping around your head? Fab. Let's get tactical in making a plan.

Now, listen. This isn't adding "one more thing to your to-do list." It's more of a wish list. Making a plan is about getting real about where and how you're going to fit *yourself* into your busy calendar.

Will all of these things happen? Um, probably not—because you're human. Are they more likely to happen because you took the time to sketch out how they could? 100 percent yes.

Divide your tool kit into categories you can break into daily, weekly, monthly, or annual commitments, then include what could serve as your accountability boost. There are three ways to think about boosting your accountability:

- **Calendar it.** Let's treat meetings with ourselves with the same integrity we'd treat a meeting at work. For example, if you want to prioritize an annual vacation, a quarterly spa day like Nneka, or just a daily walk, physically book the space on your calendar.

- **Change your physical space.** If working out and eating healthy is a priority, do you need to physically buy new shoes and better groceries? On the flip side, do you need to remove yourself from certain environments to achieve your goals? For example, to make good on my emotional self-care of taking a "Tech Shabbat"—that's going phone-free every Friday evening through Saturday evening—I literally have to turn my phone off and put it away in a drawer.

- **Connect with someone else.** One of the best ways to get an accountability boost is by asking somebody else to hold us accountable. If you have a goal that is important to you, who is somebody you trust to support it?

#5. Take (Real) Time Off. I have a rule in my coaching practice that nobody is allowed to tell me they're burned out when they haven't taken a vacation. Too often, I hear from women that life is "too busy" or their jobs are "too demanding" to make this "worth it." The prevailing logic being that it will "just be so much worse when I come back and need to catch up"—and actively contributing to the 700 million vacation days that go unused by Americans each year. Let me be clear: that is a travesty, and your paid vacation time is part of your compensation package.

Just like those micro-moments of self-care on a daily basis, that vacation can have a major impact on our performance. According to Dr. Whillans, on the other side of a vacation, we can see big boosts in our creativity (up to 33 percent), our happiness (up to 25 percent), and even our productivity (up to 13 percent).

Here's the catch: it doesn't work if you go on vacation but spend time checking or "just filing" emails anyway.

"Working on vacation," Dr. Whillans explains, "increases stress and creates time confetti, forcing employees to jump between worlds and mindsets." Vacations, she also cautions, must be part of a larger wellbeing strategy. They are not a silver bullet: "After two weeks, our after-vacation, blissed-out feeling evaporates and we go back to being over-scheduled, overcommitted, and burned out."

That's why they must be part of a more robust commitment to prioritizing daily and weekly self-care, setting boundaries, and checking some of your perfectionism or productivity bad habits (by the way, don't shoot the messenger; this *is* hard work, but important work nonetheless).

#6. Evaluate if You Have a "Job Mismatch." Okay, I share this one with a grain of salt and words of caution because I've seen too many women burn themselves out telling me their workplaces are too inflexible to make time for self-care when it's their attitudes about self-care that have been inflexible. However, if you have tried all five tools above, and it's just not working, it's time to think about if you have what Dr. Maslach calls a "job mismatch."

This means that you've used your self-care tools (consistently and with accountability), you've used your productivity and boundary tools, and you are still chronically stressed, exhausted, or burned out. A job mismatch isn't just about you or your industry/job/environment. It's about

the *relationship* between those things. Here are six categories she has studied for evaluating if you have a potential
mismatch:

#1. Workload: A mismatch can happen when
demands are consistently high and resources are
consistently low: "lots to do, but not enough time or
people or tools or information to get it done." A match
should feel more balanced on a consistent basis.

#2. Control: A match is about having choice and
discretion to handle your workload and projects on
your own (reasonable) terms. If you don't have this
basic agency, Dr. Maslach explains, "that's a huge one"
when it comes to feeling like you're in a mismatch.

#3. Reward: This is actually a tricky one. Even if the
"pay and perks per se" are great, but recognition and
"getting those social and intrinsic rewards for doing
a good job is low," that can be a sign that you have a
mismatch.

#4. Community: Dr. Maslach suggests you ask yourself, are your workplace relationships and community
"supportive in figuring out how to work out problems
and do things better? Or is it a really toxic environment where you feel that you're going to be bullied,
treated badly or kept out of things?" The latter may
suggest a mismatch.

#5. Fairness: This has to do with the "basic human need to be treated fairly in whatever the system is... Being treated unfairly [and] this is where we talk about glass ceilings, discrimination, or people getting ahead by lying and cheating rather than actually deserving of something." If you work in a place that makes you feel disrespected, Dr. Malsach explains, "That can lead to a lot of the cynicism that we see with burnout."

#6. Values and Meaning of Work: This is as simple as: Does your work feel right? Is it impactful and in line with your values? Or does it feel wrong? "Wrong" might look like an environment of conflicts, unethical behavior, or being asked to do things that you just feel are wrong in some way.

Maslach explains that when an employee has a job mismatch, it doesn't mean they should necessarily quit. But a mismatch is "problematic and raises the risk of burnout." Evaluating a mismatch is a great way to evaluate your relationship with your job and, hopefully, empower you to redesign that relationship (if possible). Before you quit your job, you must quit your bad habits.

Again, I caution you to not make this a zero-sum game of either, "I can feel awesome all the time" or, "I'm stuck with exactly how things are today." I'm asking you instead to consider making self-care one of your #1 goals. If you're not, you're probably leaving a lot on the table when it comes to your ideas, goals, and general day-to-day quality of life. Wellbeing is both critical to our success and intrinsic to a life worth living.

CONCLUSION

"Doesn't anybody notice this? I feel like I'm taking crazy pills!"

That was all I could think as I was finishing this manuscript when news broke in May 2022 of the US women's soccer team and their "historic" pay raise. I was thrilled for the women of US Soccer, but stunned by—and then *downright angry* about—the rainbows-and-butterflies news coverage of this story.

While the world seemed to be high-fiving all over the internet, all I could think about was that scene in Zoolander. You know the one: where Mugato (played to perfection by Will Ferrell) screams on a fashion runway just after the plan to assassinate the Prime Minister of Micronesia is thwarted, insanity ensues, and nobody takes note?

That's because, once again, insanity ensued for women at work, and nobody took note. In fact, the "girl power" media narrative actively contributed to the insanity when after a protracted six-year dispute over pay equity, the US Soccer Federation suddenly settled with its women players.

WHY WAS THIS PURE INSANITY?

I'm so glad you asked! To refresh your memory on the story, not only had the US women's soccer team proven that they could consistently outperform the men's team on the World Cup stage, but in 2019, they also began generating more revenue.

So their reward after six years of fighting *and* out-performing their male colleagues was… equal pay?

I read the coverage again… and again… and again, but it just didn't make any sense to me when I looked at the metrics:

- Better World Cup performance? *Check.*
- Better revenue? *Check.*
- Better popularity? *Check.*

So shouldn't they actually be making *more* than the men?

As coverage ran rampant with headlines about the team's "historic pay raise," I felt like *I* was the one on crazy pills when I opened up my newsfeed or the newspaper that arrived at my door daily.

The US women's soccer team had not received a historic raise, as it was heralded. At best, they got right-sized—and even that's a generous assessment.

What's the difference? A raise is a merit-based increase rewarding outstanding performance. A right-sizing is a realignment of compensation to accurately reflect current responsibilities and performance.

It was so clear to me that these women were still being undervalued by the media frenzy, which was telling an incomplete story. And it was a story that was distracting us from the more challenging and nuanced conversation about pay equity at hand.

Yes, we certainly needed to celebrate the tenacity of these women for standing up for what was rightfully theirs—and putting everything on the line while they fought for it for six difficult years.

We also need to make sure that we're crystal clear on another fact: a deal giving them "identical economic terms" to their male counterparts is the absolute, positive bare minimum that US Soccer could have done.

You'd think there would be some humility, but when I read a comment from US Soccer's president in *The New York Times*, I nearly fell out of my seat: "It wasn't an easy process to get to this point for sure. The most important thing here is that we are moving forward, and we are moving forward together."

"Wait," I thought, "are you telling me it was *hard* to compensate your highest performers as well as your lowest performers?"

We must keep asking these questions because US Soccer is not the only organization out there getting top female talent at a discount. This is just table stakes because it's impacting how you're able to move through your career and how you're able to live your life. This idea that we should be grateful for what we have or for the most marginal improvements, as the media insinuated the women of US Soccer should be, is a classic trope of the Old Playbook.

BACK TO THE METRICS:

That's exactly why it's critical to remember that what happened to the women of US Soccer isn't a bug in our system—it's a feature. Look no further than the numbers themselves:

82: The cents on the dollar a working woman makes compared to a man, according to the Department of Labor.

78: The cents on the dollar a woman entrepreneur makes compared to a man, according to *INC.* magazine.

69: The cents on the dollar a working mom makes as compared to a working dad, according to the National Women's Law Center.

135.6: The years the World Economic Forum predicts it will take to achieve gender pay equity at the current course and speed.

42,300,000: The estimated number of working-age women of color in the United States, according to the Institute for Women's Policy Research, for whom each one of the aforementioned gaps widens.

We must stop treating talented, high-performing women like a great find on designer jeans at Loehmann's. We are not a deal on denim. We're the future.

Unfortunately, situations like this are far too common in our current work world. They're part of the reason the Old Playbook of checking the boxes, asking for permission for our seat at the table, and having to say "thank you" for the bare minimum of respect and compensation aren't working.

They're also a battle cry and the reason why we need a New Playbook—one that can empower us to pursue our dreams and achieve our goals in this turbulent period of culture wars and shifting workplace norms. We're aching for this change, and we're demanding this change, but it's just not happening fast enough.

THE WAY FORWARD

On the morning that I was reading the US Soccer settlement coverage over breakfast, a headline in *The Washington Post* jumped out at me: "It took a revolution, but the U.S. women's soccer team got what it deserved."

I have got to have another cup of coffee if I'm going to deal with this, I thought, getting up to refresh my *Shh, There's Really Wine Inside Here* mug.

As I walked back from the kitchen into the dining room, I saw the two large pictures of the Supreme Court Justice Ruth Bader Ginsburg that hang over our credenza. Black-and-white portraits, spray-painted on butcher paper and stenciled with the words "RIP RBG," they're two of the sixty prints the DC-based street artist AbsurdlyWell made after the Justice passed away on September 18, 2020.

Over three feet tall each, I looked up at a towering RBG: the Patron Saint of women everywhere managing to kill the game in a system designed more for our failure than our success.

As I sat, sipping my coffee and letting my blood pressure come down, I found myself thinking less about crazy pills and more about her legacy. Famous for chipping away at the wall of gender bias instead of toppling it, Ginsburg taught us the power of winning the war by winning small battles.

Yes, the media missed the mark. Before I'd have the opportunity to say my piece about this a few weeks later in *Forbes*, I harkened back to her sage wisdom that morning. "I'm dejected, but only momentarily, when I can't get the fifth vote for something I think is very important," Ginsburg had said about the need to look forward. "There'll be another time, another day."

I continued sipping my coffee under the careful watch of the late, great Justice, scrolling onto another interview with US women's soccer player, Midge Purce. *She nailed it,* I thought when she told *The Wall Street Journal* what this means for the next generation: "I feel a lot of pride that there are a lot of young girls who are going to see what we've accomplished and grow up recognizing their value rather than fighting to find it."

Purce reminded us that the world is changing before our very eyes—but not quickly enough. The US women's soccer team's settlement is a reminder that we're living through the end of the beginning. We're nowhere near the beginning of the end.

We have a taste of what's possible, and that's why I hope we will all use our voices (and our votes) to continue to make change with each other—and for each other. That's also why I hope the New Playbook will arm you with the tools you need to create, define, and enjoy success on your terms—especially while our workplaces (and culture at large) remain a work in progress on their best days and a total dumpster fire on their worst ones.

As we continue to claim our place, our successes, and our stories, some will criticize us and say, "It's never enough." Purce reminds us, however, that there are women and girls out there who have dreams that just can't wait 135 years for the pay gap to close.

I'm one of them, and I suspect that you are, too. That's why I look forward to the day when this book is an outdated relic of a bygone era, collecting dust on a shelf, and irrelevant in a world that has been designed to truly advance women— *all* women—at work.

Still, you might wonder, I just talked about crazy pills. How could I still possibly be bullish on the future for women at work? I look no further than US women's soccer star, Megan Rapinoe, herself.

I first started writing about her quest for equal pay on behalf of the US women's soccer team years ago, when I started my business. How timely then that mere days before this manuscript was due, she would be awarded the Presidential Medal of Freedom for her relentless fight for pay equity.

"For us," she told *The Today Show*, "this is just a huge win in ensuring that we not only right the wrongs of the past, but set the next generation up for something we only dreamed of."

"It's pretty on par with [Rapinoe] to get one of the most amazing awards ever and then immediately say it's a team award," teammate Becky Sauerbrunn tearfully told *The Los Angeles Times* after news broke of Rapinoe receiving the Presidential Medal of Freedom. "That's just how she is," she added. "This team has always had a legacy of fighting for things off the field to make society better than what it is. And unfortunately, there's always going to be things that we're going to be fighting for."

Let's celebrate the wins—and never take our eyes off the ball.

ACKNOWLEDGMENTS

There are so many people I want to thank for helping me bring this book to fruition, starting with my editorial dream team: thanks to my developmental editor, John Palisano, for helping me get these ideas out of my brain and onto the page and for mentoring me on the art of story-telling. Thanks to Sara Stibitz, my revisions editor, and her assistant Faith Smith-Place, for helping me refine this book and for challenging me to hone its core messages: this book is what it is because your fingerprints are on it, Sara. Lastly, thanks to Shanna Heath for being my editorial fairy godmother and to my research assistant, Hannah Seligman, for her diligent work helping me organize all the research that went into this manuscript.

It's the songbirds that make this book sing, and I'm so grateful for all the women who shared stories in this book and who have trusted me over the years with their goals and dreams as their coach: I will not name names to protect anonymity, but know that I offer my deepest gratitude to each and every one of you.

Thank you to my team at Something Major—Jeanine, Faleign, Johnny, Brittany, Jess, Carlee, and Renee. I only realized this project with all of your support, and thanks for making work magical.

Thanks also to my mentors for all of your support: to Michael Berenbaum for "interventioning" me to finally write this book in your backyard in Los Angeles, to Ken Mossman for seeing me as a "force of nature," and to my own longtime coach, LA Redding, for being my partner in crime on this project and so much more.

I have immense appreciation for the early readers of this manuscript: Bonnie, Dana, Kate, Lanie, Laurea, Nikki, Megan, Meredith, and Vonetta. Thank you all for being so generous with your time and feedback.

Finally, I'd like to thank my family: to my found family, thank you Mer, Dan, and Megan for being the best friends anybody could ask for.

Thanks to my late Grandma Gloria and Grandma Fifi who wrote their *own* playbooks as women at work—both so ahead of their times. Thanks to Sandra and Bob for keeping the wine flowing while I finished the first draft of this book in your backyard, to Charlie and Jonah for cheering me on, and to Lanie for both being such a source of support and for teaching me the art of a good storyboard.

Thank you, Mom, for modeling what it can look like to love your family and your career, and thank you, Dad, for teaching me to always believe in myself. Thanks to my sweet babes—to Fifi, for championing me every step of the way and for helping me make my storyboards, and to Theo, for being my "research assistant."

Last—but never least—thank you to my best friend and husband, Benjy, for... *literally everything.* You've made my life an adventure since I was nineteen, and this was one for the books. It's "all part of the story," and I love you.

BIBLIOGRAPHY

———

INTRODUCTION

Buchholz, Katharina. "How has the number of female CEOs in Fortune 500 companies changed over the last 20 years?" World Economic Forum. 10 Mar 2022. https://www.weforum.org/agenda/2022/03/ceos-fortune-500-companies-female#:~:text=As%20of%20March%2C%20there%20were,and%20only%207%20in%202002.

Connley, Courtney. "A Record 41 Women Are Fortune 500 Ceos—and for the First Time Two Black Women Made the List." *CNBC*, 2 Jun 2021. https://www.cnbc.com/2021/06/02/fortune-500-now-has-a-record-41-women-running-companies.html.

Green, Jeff. "Male Executives Control 99 Times More S&P 500 Shares than Women." *The Jerusalem Post*, 7 Jun 2022. https://www.jpost.com/business-and-innovation/all-news/article-708765?utm_source=jpost.app.apple&utm_medium=share.

Green, Jeff. "S&P 500 Companies up Boardroom Diversity with Record Black Women Hold Seats." *Bloomberg*. 22 Dec 2021. https://www.bloomberg.com/news/articles/2021-12-22/black-

women-hold-record-share-of-s-p-500-boardroom-seats#:~:-
text=The%20number%20of%20S%26P%20500,board%20
seats%2C%20the%20data%20show.

Guynn, Jessica and Jayme Fraser. "Corporate Boards Used to
Be Mostly White and Male. That's Changed since George
Floyd's Murder." *USA Today*, 31 May 2022. https://www.usa-
today.com/story/money/2022/05/31/corporate-board-diver-
sity-george-floyd/9948384002/?gnt-cfr=1.

Hinchliffe, Emma. "The Female CEOs on This Year's Fortune
500 Just Broke Three All-Time Records." *Fortune*, 2 Jun 2021.
https://fortune.com/2021/06/02/female-ceos-fortune-500-
2021-women-ceo-list-roz-brewer-walgreens-karen-lynch-
cvs-thasunda-brown-duckett-tiaa/.

Huang, Georgene. "Women Are Losing Confidence at Work
– Here's How to Help Them in 2022." *Forbes*, 3 Jan 2022.
https://www.forbes.com/sites/georgenehuang/2022/01/03/
women-are-losing-confidence-at-work--heres-how-to-help-
them-in-2022/?sh=d1ea79a38b69.

Lacey, Natalie and Darrell Bricker. "The COVID-19 effect on
the global gender gap: Measuring it is the first step toward
closing it." World Economic Forum. 31 Mar 2021. https://
www.weforum.org/agenda/2021/03/the-covid-19-effect-on-
the-global-gender-gap-measuring-it-is-the-first-step-to-
ward-closing-it/.

Ohikuare, Judith. "Best Ruth Bader Ginsburg Quotes On Her
85th Birthday." *Refinery29*, 15 Mar 2018. https://www.refin-
ery29.com/en-us/2018/03/191666/best-ruth-bader-ginsburg-
quotes#slide-3.

Orgad, Shani and Rosalind Gill. *Confidence Culture.* Duke University Press, 2022, p. 2–6.

Parmelee, Michelle and Emma Codd. "Women at Work 2022."
Deloitte Global. 26 Apr 2022. https://www2.deloitte.com/

global/en/pages/about-deloitte/articles/women-at-work-global-outlook.htm.

Rahilly, Lucia, host. "Women Leaders Continue to Feel the Burn of Burnout." *The McKinsey Podcast*, McKinsey & Company, 4 Jan 2022. https://www.mckinsey.com/featured-insights/coronavirus-leading-through-the-crisis/charting-the-path-to-the-next-normal/women-leaders-continue-to-feel-the-burn-of-burnout.

Safronova, Valeriya. "Is Confidence the Secret to Success? Not Exactly." *The New York Times*, 7 Feb 2022. https://www.nytimes.com/2022/02/07/style/confidence-culture-book.html.

Thomas, Rachel, et al. "Women in the Workplace 2022." Lean In and McKinsey & Co. 18 Oct 2022, p. 7. https://wiw-report.s3.amazonaws.com/Women_in_the_Workplace_2022.pdf.

Tucker, Jasmine and Brooke LePage. "The Jobs Report Shows a Strong Month, but Black Women's Labor Force Participation Drops and Unemployment Rate Rises." National Women's Law Center. 4 Mar 2022. https://nwlc.org/resource/the-jobs-report-shows-a-strong-month-but-black-womens-labor-force-participation-drops-and-unemployment-rate-rises/.

CHAPTER 1: DITCHING PERFECTIONISM

Ablard, Karen E. and Rachelle E. Lipschultz. "Self-Regulated Learning in High-Achieving Students: Relations to Advanced Reasoning, Achievement Goals, and Gender." *Journal of Educational Psychology*, Vol 90 no. 1, Mar 1998, p. 94–101. http://psycnet.apa.org/fulltext/1998-00166-008.pdf.

Brown, Brené. *The Gifts of Imperfection: Let Go of Who You Think You're Supposed to Be and Embrace Who You Are.* Hazelden, 2010, p. 55–58.

Carmichael, Sarah Green, Amy Bernstein, and Nicole Torres, hosts. "Let's Do Less Dead-End Work with Lise Verstlund." *Women at Work*, Season 2, Episode 1, Harvard Business Review. 17 Sept 2018. https://hbr.org/podcast/2018/09/lets-do-less-dead-end-work.

Damour, Lisa. "Why Girls Beat Boys at School and Lose to Them at the Office." *The New York Times*, 7 Feb 2019. https://www.nytimes.com/2019/02/07/opinion/sunday/girls-school-confidence.html.

Duckworth, Angela Lee and Martin E. P. Seligman. "Gender in Self-Discipline, Grades, and Achievement Test Scores." *Journal of Educational Psychology*, Vol 98 no. 1, Feb 2006, p. 198–208. http://psycnet.apa.org/fulltext/2006-02666-016.pdf.

Duckworth, Angela L., et al. "Will Not Want: Self-Control Rather than Motivation Explains the Female Advantage in Report Card Grades." *Learning and individual differences* vol. 39, Apr 2015, p. 13–23. https://www.ncbi.nlm.nih.gov/pmc/articles/PMC4395866/.

Fortin, Nicole M., Philip Oreopoulos, and Shelley Phipps. "Leaving Boys Behind: Gender Disparities in High Academic Achievement." National Bureau of Economic Research, NBER Working Paper Series. Aug 2013. https://www.nber.org/papers/w19331.pdf.

Lakshmin, Pooja. "How Society Has Turned Its Back on Mothers." *The New York Times*, 4 Feb 2021. https://www.nytimes.com/2021/02/04/parenting/working-mom-burnout-coronavirus.html.

Mishra, Subodh. "Women in the C-Suite: The Next Frontier in Gender Diversity." Harvard Law School Forum on Corporate Governance. 13 Aug 2018. https://corpgov.law.harvard.edu/2018/08/13/women-in-the-c-suite-the-next-frontier-in-gender-diversity/.

Obama, Michelle. "A Conversation with Michelle Obama." CHIEF. February 15, 2022. Virtual Lecture.

Wang, Yang, Benjamin F. Jones, and Dashun Wang. "Early Career Failures Can Make You Stronger in the Long Run." Kellogg Insight. October 1 2019. https://insight.kellogg.northwestern.edu/article/early-setbacks-failure-career-success.

Wasserman, Claire. Zoom Interview. May 17, 2022.

Watanabe, Teresa. "College Admission Season Wraps up with a Rejection Party, a Paper Shredder and Joy." *Los Angeles Times*, 15 Apr 2022. https://www.latimes.com/california/story/2022-04-15/college-admission-season-ends-acceptance-rejection.

Williams, Joan C. and Marina Multhaup. "For Women and Minorities to Get Ahead, Managers Must Assign Work Fairly." *Harvard Business Review*, 5 Mar 2018. https://hbr.org/2018/03/for-women-and-minorities-to-get-ahead-managers-must-assign-work-fairly.

Wong, Ali. *Dear Girls: Intimate Tales, Untold Secrets, & Advice for Living Your Best Life.* Random House, 2019, p. 51–56.

Walravens, Samantha. "Why Girls Lead In The Classroom, But Not In The Boardroom." *Forbes*, 04 Aug 2020. https://www.forbes.com/sites/geekgirlrising/2020/08/04/why-girls-lead-in-the-classroom-but-not-in-the-boardroom/

CHAPTER 2: UNTETHERING FROM EXTERNAL VALIDATION

Berinato, Scott. "Negative Feedback Rarely Leads to Improvement." *Harvard Business Review Magazine*, Jan-Feb 2018. https://hbr.org/2018/01/negative-feedback-rarely-leads-to-improvement.

Grant, Adam, host. "When Strength Becomes Weakness with Marcus Buckingham." *WorkLife with Adam Grant*, Season

2, Episode 1, TED. https://www.ted.com/talks/worklife_
with_adam_grant_when_strength_becomes_weakness/
transcript?language=en.

Inside Edition. "Why 'Seinfeld' Almost Didn't Become a TV
Show." *Inside Edition*, 29 Jun 2015. https://www.insideedition.
com/10941-why-seinfeld-almost-didnt-become-a-tv-show.

Losada, Marcial, and Emily Heaphy. "The Role of Positivity and
Connectivity in the Performance of Business Teams: A Non-
linear Dynamics Model." *American Behavioral Scientist*, vol.
47, no. 6, Feb. 2004, p. 740–765. https://journals.sagepub.com/
doi/pdf/10.1177/0002764203260208.

Low-Kramen, Bonnie. Zoom Interview. June 29, 2022.

Miranda, Lin-Manuel. "Lin-Manuel Miranda Recalls His
Nerve-Wracking Hamilton Performance for the Obamas."
The Tonight Show Starring Jimmy Fallon, hosted by Jimmy
Fallon, NBC, 23 Jun 2020. https://www.youtube.com/
watch?v=wWk5U9cKkg8.

O'Brien, Conan, host. "Lin-Manuel Miranda." *Conan O'Brien
Needs a Friend*, Season 1, Episode 31, Team Coco & Earworm,
16 Jun 2019. https://podcasts.apple.com/us/podcast/lin-man-
uel-miranda/id1438054347?i=1000441752668.

Rigoni, Brandon and Jim Asplund. "Strengths-Based
Employee Development: The Business Results." Gallup.
7 Jul 2016. https://www.gallup.com/workplace/236297/
strengths-based-employee-development-business-results.
aspx.

Van Ness, Jonathan. *Love That Story: Observations from a Gorgeously Queer Life*. HarperOne, 2022, p. 18.

Zenger, Jack and Joseph Folkman. "The Ideal Praise-to-Criticism
Ratio." *Harvard Business Review*. 15 Mar 2013. https://hbr.
org/2013/03/the-ideal-praise-to-criticism#:~:text=And%20

the%20optimal%20ratio%20is,their%20place%20and%20
their%20time.

CHAPTER 3: QUIETING OUR INNER CRITIC

Bateman, Aimee. "Judgment. Don't Let It Frighten You | Aimee Bateman | TEDxClapham." YouTube, uploaded by TEDx Talks, 19 Feb 2015. https://www.youtube.com/watch?v=wBTEJsDP-nU.

Brown, Brené. *The Gifts of Imperfection: Let Go of Who You Think You're Supposed to Be and Embrace Who You Are.* Hazelden, 2010, p. 67.

Dufu, Tiffany. *Drop the Ball: Achieving More by Doing Less.* Flatiron Books, 2017, p. 36.

Grant, Adam. "A Conversation with Adam Grant." CHIEF. December 6, 2021. Virtual Lecture.

Kelly, Matt. "Joe Sewell strikes out twice in game for first time." Baseball Hall of Fame. https://baseballhall.org/discover-more/stories/inside-pitch/joe-sewell-strikes-out-twice-in-one-game-for-first-time.

Mohr, Tara. *Playing Big: Practical Wisdom for Women Who Want to Speak Up, Create, and Lead.* Penguin, 2014, p. 4–6, 15, 21.

Obama, Michelle. "A Conversation with Michelle Obama." CHIEF. February 15, 2022. Virtual Lecture.

Ruth, Babe. "Famous Quotes by Babe Ruth." http://www.babe-ruth.com/quotes/.

Tulshyan, Ruchika and Jodi-Ann Burey. "Stop Telling Women They Have Imposter Syndrome." *Harvard Business Review.* 11 Feb 2021, https://hbr.org/2021/02/stop-telling-women-they-have-imposter-syndrome.

CHAPTER 4: RECLAIMING OUR INTUITION

Blakely, Sara. "Sara Blakely in The Power Seat." CHIEF. January 31, 2021. Virtual Lecture.

Brown, Brené. *The Gifts of Imperfection: Let Go of Who You Think You're Supposed to Be and Embrace Who You Are.* Hazelden, 2010, p. 87–90.

Grant, Adam. *Think Again.* Viking, 2021. p. 38–39.

Haverstock, Eliza. "Sara Blakely Is A Billionaire (Again) After Selling A Majority Of Spanx To Blackstone." *Forbes*, 20 Oct 2021. https://www.forbes.com/sites/elizahaverstock/2021/10/20/sara-blakely-is-a-billionaire-again-after-selling-a-majority-of-spanx-to-blackstone/?sh=1e89a5887d5c.

Kahneman, Daniel. *Thinking Fast and Slow.* Farrar, Strauss and Giroux, 2011, p. 21–22, 48.

Obama, Michelle. "A Conversation with Michelle Obama." CHIEF. February 15, 2022. Virtual Lecture.

Tessler, Bari. *The Art of Money: A Life-Changing Guide to Financial Happiness.* Parallax Press, 2016, p. 51–52.

The Johns Hopkins Hospital. "The Brain-Gut Connection." Johns Hopkins Medicine. Accessed October 25, 2022. https://www.hopkinsmedicine.org/health/wellness-and-prevention/the-brain-gut-connection.

CHAPTER 5: GETTING AFTER YOUR GOALS

Harrell, Eben. "How 1% Performance Improvements Led to Olympic Gold." *Harvard Business Review*, 30 Oct 2015. https://hbr.org/2015/10/how-1-performance-improvements-led-to-olympic-gold.

Jay, Meg. "Why 30 Is Not the New 20." *TED*, May 2013. https://www.ted.com/talks/meg_jay_why_30_is_not_the_new_20/transcript.

Mackelden, Amy. "Ruth Bader Ginsburg's Most Inspiring Quotes About Feminism." *Harper's Bazaar*, 19 Sept 2020. https://www.harpersbazaar.com/culture/politics/a34083262/ruth-bader-ginsburg-inspiring-quotes/.

Myers, Joe. "This Coach Improved Everything by 1%. This Is the Remarkable Difference It's Made." World Economic Forum, 17 Aug 2016. https://www.weforum.org/agenda/2016/08/this-coach-improved-everything-by-1-this-is-the-remarkable-difference-it-s-made/.

Norton, Kat. "This 28-Year-Old Quit Her Job to Pursue Her Side Hustle." *CNBC*, 2 Feb 2022. https://www.cnbc.com/2022/02/02/this-28-year-old-turned-her-side-hustle-into-a-million-dollar-business-and-made-100000-in-passive-income.html.

Patel, Nilay host. "How an Excel TikToker Manifested Her Way to Making Six Figures a Day." *Decoder*, The Verge, 30 Nov 2021. https://www.theverge.com/22807858/tiktok-influencer-microsoft-excel-instagram-decoder-podcast.

CHAPTER 6: REBOUNDING WHEN THE PLAN BLOWS UP

Alter, Charlotte. "How Whitney Wolfe Herd Made Bumble a Billion-Dollar Brand." *Time*, 19 Mar 2021. https://time.com/5947727/whitney-wolfe-herd-bumble/.

Alter, Charlotte. "Whitney Wolfe Wants to Beat Tinder at Its Own Game." *Time*, 15 May 2015. https://time.com/3851583/bumble-whitney-wolfe/.

Arzón, Robin. "A Fireside Chat with Robin Arzón." CHIEF. June 19, 2021. Virtual Lecture.

Baker, Al. "Man Shoots 3 In Rampage In East Village." *New York Times*, 17 Jun 2002. https://www.nytimes.com/2002/06/17/nyregion/man-shoots-3-in-rampage-in-east-village.html.

Berra, Lindsay. "How Robin Arzon, a Former Non-athlete, Became the Face of Fitness for Cycling Superpower Peloton." *ESPN*, 23 May 2019. https://www.espn.com/espnw/life-style/article/26808750/how-robin-arzon-former-non-athlete-became-face-fitness-cycling-superpower-peloton.

Brown, Brené. *The Gifts of Imperfection: Let Go of Who You Think You're Supposed to Be and Embrace Who You Are.* Hazelden, 2010, p. 12.

Frankl, Viktor. *Man's Search for Meaning.* Beacon Press, 2006, p. 111–112.

Grant, Adam, host. "When Strength Becomes Weakness with Marcus Buckingham." *WorkLife with Adam Grant*, Season 2, Episode 1, TED. https://www.ted.com/talks/worklife_with_adam_grant_when_strength_becomes_weakness/transcript?language=en.

Grant, Adam. *Think Again.* Viking, 2021, p. 233.

Hinchliffe, Emma. "Bumble CEO Whitney Wolfe Herd Becomes the Youngest Woman to Take a Company Public." *Fortune*, 11 Feb 2021. https://fortune.com/2021/02/11/bumble-ipo-ceo-whitney-wolfe-herd-bmbl-stock-shares-interview-app-initial-public-offering/.

Hollis, Rachel, host. "99: Learning by Doing with Robin Arzon." *The Rachel Hollis Podcast*, Episode 99, RISE Podcast, 4 Jun 2019. https://podcasts.apple.com/us/podcast/99-learning-by-doing-with-robin-arzon/id1245763628?i=1000440570275.

"Identity foreclosure." APA Dictionary of Psychology, American Psychological Association. https://dictionary.apa.org/identity-foreclosure.

Kurutz, Steven. "Peloton Instructors Ride for Fitness and Fame." *New York Times*, 1 Feb 2017. https://www.nytimes.com/2017/02/01/style/peloton-fitness-cycling-celebrity-instructors.html.

Lashinsky, Adam. "23 minutes with Peloton's Robin Arzón." *Fortune*, 15 Jun 2020. https://fortune.com/2020/06/15/robin-arzon-peloton-interview-fitness-workout-quotes/.

Mandela, Nelson. "Nelson Mandela's Most Powerful Quotes." *BET*, 5 Dec 2013. https://www.bet.com/photo-gallery/8i8zbz/nelson-mandela-s-most-powerful-quotes/vyp3ag.

Ohikuare, Judith. "Best Ruth Bader Ginsburg Quotes On Her 85th Birthday." *Refinery29*, 15 Mar 2018. https://www.refinery29.com/en-us/2018/03/191666/best-ruth-bader-ginsburg-quotes#slide-3.

Oliver, Claire. "Peloton VP Robin Arzón Talks About Taking the Biggest Career Risk of Her Life—and How It Paid Off." CHIEF. 26 Jul 2021. https://chief.com/articles/robin-arzon.

"Robin Arzón | 2020 40 under 40 in Media and Entertainment." *Fortune*, 2 Sept 2020. https://fortune.com/40-under-40/2020/robin-arzon/.

Thomas, Lauren. "Peloton Thinks It Can Grow To 100 Million Subscribers. Here's How." *CNBC*, 15 Sept 2020. https://www.cnbc.com/2020/09/15/peloton-thinks-it-can-grow-to-100-million-subscribers-heres-how.html.

CHAPTER 7: OWNING YOUR MESSAGE

Brescoll, Victoria L. "Who Takes the Floor and Why: Gender, Power, and Volubility in Organizations." *Administrative Science Quarterly*, vol. 56, no. 4, Dec. 2011, pp. 622–641. https://journals.sagepub.com/doi/abs/10.1177/0001839212439994.

Dixon, Matt. Zoom Interview. June 15, 2022.

Eilperin, Juliet. "White House Women Want to Be in the Room Where It Happens." *Washington Post*, 13 Sept 2016. https://www.washingtonpost.com/news/powerpost/wp/2016/09/13/white-house-women-are-now-in-the-room-where-it-happens/.

Fineman, Meredith. *Brag Better: Master the Art of Fearless Self-Promotion*. Penguin Random House, 2020, pgs. 3, 6, 8, 9, 16.

Gino, Francesca. "The Business Case for Curiosity." *Harvard Business Review Magazine*, Sept-Oct 2018. https://hbr.org/2018/09/the-business-case-for-curiosity.

Hancock, Adrienne B., and Benjamin A. Rubin. "Influence of Communication Partner's Gender on Language." *Journal of Language and Social Psychology*, vol. 34, no. 1, Jan. 2015, pp. 46–64. https://journals.sagepub.com/doi/abs/10.1177/0261927X14533197?papetoc=&.

Kim, Larry. "Avoid This One Punctuation Habit That Will Destroy Your Credibility (Infographic)." Inc.com, 17 Feb 2015. https://www.inc.com/larry-kim/avoid-this-one-punctuation-habit-that-will-destroy-your-credibility.html.

Michel-Carter, Christine. Zoom Interview. June 1, 2022.

Moyers, Stephen. "How Email Attention Span is Increasing." Sphinx Digital. https://www.spinxdigital.com/blog/how-email-attention-span-is-increasing/#:~:text=According%20to%20Litmus'%20research%2C%20the,emails%20compared%20to%202011%20rates.

Rich, Natalie. "The 'Yes-Damn' Effect." *UNC Healthy Heels.* 27 Jan 2012. https://healthyheels.org/2012/01/27/the-yes-damn-effect/.

Sandberg, Sheryl and Adam Grant. "Speaking While Female." *New York Times*, 12 Jan 2015. https://www.nytimes.com/2015/01/11/opinion/sunday/speaking-while-female.html?_r=0.

"States with Salary History Bans." Paycor. 2 Dec 2020. https://www.paycor.com/resource-center/articles/states-with-salary-history-bans/.

CHAPTER 8: REASSESSING PRODUCTIVITY & RECLAIMING TIME

Adesiyan, Blessing. "We Need to Dismantle the Productivity Lie That Demands We 'Do It All'." Fast Company. 6 Dec 2021. https://www.fastcompany.com/90702605/we-need-to-dismantle-the-productivity-lie-that-demands-we-do-it-all.

Adesiyan, Blessing. Zoom Interview. June 10, 2022.

Giurge, Laura M. and Vanessa K. Bohns. "You Don't Need to Answer Right Away! Receivers Overestimate How Quickly Senders Expect Responses to Non-urgent Work Emails." *Organizational Behavior and Human Decision Processes*, Volume 167, Nov 2021, p. 114–128. https://www.sciencedirect.com/science/article/abs/pii/S0749597821000807.

Liu, Jennifer. "People Spend More than Half of the Day on Busy Work, Says Asana Survey." *CNBC*, 6 Apr 2022. https://www.cnbc.com/2022/04/06/people-spend-more-than-half-of-the-day-on-busy-work-says-asana-survey.html.

Pinsker, Joe. "What If We Just Stop Being So Available?" *The Atlantic*, 14 Jan 2022. https://www.theatlantic.com/family/archive/2022/01/not-sorry-for-my-delay/621264/?mc_cid=f-70084238b&mc_eid=3794df7edc

Rodsky, Eve. "Find Your Unicorn Space." Mother Honestly. January 21, 2021. Virtual Lecture.

Tagle, Andee. "22 Tips for 2022: If You Want to Succeed, Choose Your Failures—in Advance." *NPR*, 9 Jan 2022. https://www.npr.org/2022/01/09/1070719110/productivity-tips.

Tucker, Jasmine and Brooke LePage. "The Jobs Report Shows a Strong Month, but Black Women's Labor Force Participation Drops and Unemployment Rate Rises." National Women's Law Center. 4 Mar 2022. https://nwlc.org/resource/the-jobs-report-shows-a-strong-month-but-black-womens-labor-force-participation-drops-and-unemployment-rate-rises/.

Whillans, Ashley. *Time Smart.* Harvard Business Review Press, Boston, 2020. p. 16–18, 26–29.

CHAPTER 9: BUILDING BOUNDARIES

Abbajay, Mary. Zoom Interview. May 25, 2022.

Biles, Simone. "Simone Biles Speaks after Withdrawing from Gymnastics Finals." YouTube, 27 Jul 2021. https://www.youtube.com/watch?v=DIS7HXBAdDU.

Gallo, Amy, Amy Bernstein, and Nicole Torres, hosts. "How We Take Care of Ourselves." *Women at Work*, Season 4, Episode 5, Harvard Business Review, 11 Nov 2018. https://hbr.org/podcast/2019/11/how-we-take-care-of-ourselves.

Gregory, Colette. Zoom Interview. June 30, 2022.

Lerner, Claire. "Working Moms Burnout Bootcamp: Practical Pandemic Parenting." Something Major. March 21, 2021. Virtual Lecture.

Rodsky, Eve. *Find Your Unicorn Space.* G.P. Putnam's Sons, New York, 2021, p. 67.

Rodsky, Eve. "Find Your Unicorn Space." Mother Honestly. January 21, 2021. Virtual Lecture.

CHAPTER 10: REIMAGINING WELLBEING

Atkins Stohr, Kimberly. "The Complicated History of Women's Fitness." *On Point*, WBUR, 18 Apr 2022. https://www.wbur.org/onpoint/2022/04/18/the-secret-history-of-womens-fitness.

Gallo, Amy, Amy Bernstein, and Nicole Torres, hosts. "How We Take Care of Ourselves." *Women at Work*, Season 4, Episode 5, Harvard Business Review, 11 Nov 2018. https://hbr.org/podcast/2019/11/how-we-take-care-of-ourselves.

Fairchild, Caroline. "Women Expect Less from Their Careers than Ever Before. Here's How We Change That." *Work-*

ing Together, LinkedIn, 8 Mar 2021. https://www.linkedin. com/pulse/women-expect-less-from-careers-than-ever-be-fore-heres-fairchild/?trackingId=aRK5%2Bjjr8esKEVajRT-wr4A%3D%3D.

Mills, Kim,host. "Why We're Burned Out and What to Do about It, with Christina Maslach, PhD." *Speaking of Psychology*, Episode 152, American Psychological Association, 28 July 2022. https://www.apa.org/news/podcasts/speaking-of-psy-chology/burnout.

Milne-Tyte, Ashley, host. "Showing Up to Work Tired Is Just Like Showing Up to Work Drunk." *Marketplace Morning Report*, Marketplace, 6 Nov 2013. https://www.marketplace. org/2013/11/06/showing-work-tired-just-showing-work-drunk/.

Pacheco, Danielle and Dr. Anis Rehman. "Do Women Need More Sleep Than Men?" Sleep Foundation. 6 May 2022. https://www.sleepfoundation.org/women-sleep/do-wom-en-need-more-sleep-than-men.

"Racism Is Bad for Your Health." Harvard T.H. Chan School of Public Health. 28 Oct 2016. https://www.hsph.harvard.edu/ news/hsph-in-the-news/racism-bad-for-health/.

Reviewed by Psychology Today Staff. "Stress." *Psychology Today*. https://www.psychologytoday.com/us/basics/stress.

Selterman, Dylan. "Dylan Selterman: What Are Our Dreams—and Nightmares—Trying to Tell Us?" *TED Radio Hour*, NPR, 18 Feb 2022. https://www.npr.org/2022/02/18/1081449528/ dylan-selterman-what-are-our-dreams-and-nightmares-trying-to-tell-us.

Suni, Eric, and Kimberly Truong. "Sleep Statistics - Facts and Data About Sleep 2022." Sleep Foundation. 13 May 2022. https://www.sleepfoundation.org/how-sleep-works/

sleep-facts-statistics#:~:text=Adults%20between%2018%20
and%2064,than%20seven%20hours%20per%20night.

"Survey Finds Disordered Eating Behaviors among Three Out of
Four American Women (Fall, 2008)." *Carolina Public Health
Magazine*, University of North Carolina Gillings School of
Global Public Health, 26 Sept 2008. https://sph.unc.edu/
cphm/carolina-public-health-magazine-accelerate-fall-2008/
survey-finds-disordered-eating-behaviors-among-three-
out-of-four-american-women-fall-2008/.

Welby, Melissa M.D. "Self-Care Isn't Rocket Science." *Psychology
Today*, 6 Oct 2019. https://www.psychologytoday.com/us/
blog/transformative-healing/201910/self-care-isnt-rocket-
science.

Whillans, Ashley. *Time Smart.* Harvard Business Review Press,
Boston, 2020. p. 128–129

CONCLUSION

Baxter, Kevin. "Megan Rapinoe: Presidential Award Is 'Validation of All the Things That I've Stood For'." *Los Angeles
Times*, 3 Jul 2022. https://www.latimes.com/sports/soc-
cer/story/2022-07-03/megan-rapinoe-presidential-med-
al-of-freedom-social-justice.

Braun, Randi. "59 Years After The Equal Pay Act, Women Still
Struggle For The Bare Minimum." *Forbes*, 12 Jul 2022. https://
www.forbes.com/sites/forbescoachescouncil/2022/07/12/59-
years-after-the-equal-pay-act-women-still-struggle-for-the-
bare-minimum/.

Braun, Randi. "Living Life According to Justice Ginsburg."
Jewish Journal, 24 Sept 2020. https://jewishjournal.com/
commentary/opinion/321993/living-life-according-to-jus-
tice-ginsburg/.

Das, Andrew. "U.S. Soccer and Top Players Agree to Guarantee Equal Pay." *New York Times*, 18 May 2022. http://nytimes. com/2022/05/18/sports/soccer/us-soccer-equal-pay-deal. html.

Haller, Sonja. "Moms Equal Pay Day: 'Shocking' Statistics Explain Why Working Moms Are So Stressed." *USA Today*, 10 Jun 2019. https://www.usatoday.com/story/life/allth-emoms/2019/06/10/wage-gap-widens-between-working-moms-and-dads-nwlc-moms-equal-pay-day/1344822001/.

Jones, Janelle. "5 Facts About the State of the Gender Pay Gap." U.S. Department of Labor Blog (blog). 19 Mar 2021. https:// blog.dol.gov/2021/03/19/5-facts-about-the-state-of-the-gen-der-pay-gap#:~:text=Women%20earn%2082%20cents%20 for,for%20many%20women%20of%20color.

Ng, Abigail. "COVID Widened the Gender Gap—It Will Now Take 135 Years to Close That Divide, WEF Says." *CNBC*, 1 Apr 2021. https://www.cnbc.com/2021/04/01/wef-covid-wors-ened-the-gender-gap-it-will-take-135-years-to-close.html.

Ohikuare, Judith. "Best Ruth Bader Ginsburg Quotes On Her 85th Birthday." *Refinery29*, 15 Mar 2018. https://www.refin-ery29.com/en-us/2018/03/191666/best-ruth-bader-ginsburg-quotes#slide-3.

Sheer, Lynn. "A Conversation with Ruth Bader Ginsburg." *The Record of Association of the Bar of the City of New York*, Volume 56, Number 1, Winter 2001, p. 20. https://www2.nycbar. org/Publications/record/winter01.1.pdf.

Stump, Scott. "Megan Rapinoe on Us Women's Soccer Team's Equal Pay Agreement: 'This Is a Huge Win'." *Today*, 22 Feb 2022. https://www.today.com/news/sports/us-womens-soccer-equal-pay-agreement-megan-rapinoe-alex-morgan-rcna17140.

Weisul, Kimberly. "When It Comes to Revenue, Women Entrepreneurs Are Pummeling the Guys." Inc.com. 6 Jun 2018. https://www.inc.com/kimberly-weisul/boston-consulting-group-female-founders-higher-revenues.html.

Williams-Baron, Emma and Elyse Shaw. "Women of Color: Where They Are in the United States." Institute for Women's Policy Research. 19 Oct 2016. https://iwpr.org/iwpr-issues/race-ethnicity-gender-and-economy/women-of-color-where-they-are-in-the-united-states/.

CPSIA information can be obtained
at www.ICGtesting.com
Printed in the USA
LVHW102147010323
740742LV00009B/56/J

9 798885 043373